MOSAICS
OF
SPAIN

BOOKS BY JASON WEBSTER

NON-FICTION

Duende: A Journey in Search of Flamenco

Andalus: Unlocking the Secrets of Moorish Spain

¡Guerra!: Living in the Shadows of the Spanish Civil War

Sacred Sierra: A Year on a Spanish Mountain

The Spy with 29 Names: The Story of the Second World War's Most Audacious Double Agent

Violencia: A New History of Spain

THE MAX CÁMARA CRIME NOVELS

Or the Bull Kills You

A Death in Valencia

The Anarchist Detective

Blood Med

A Body in Barcelona

Fatal Sunset

THE WORLD OF MAX CÁMARA

MOSAICS OF SPAIN VOLUME I

JASON WEBSTER

CORSARIO

CORSARIO

www.corsariobooks.com
info@corsariobooks.com

First published by Corsario, 2020

THE WORLD OF MAX CÁMARA
MOSAICS OF SPAIN VOLUME I

Copyright © Jason Webster

www.jasonwebster.net

The right of Jason Webster to be identified
as the owner of this work has been asserted by them in accordance
with the Copyright, Designs and Patents Act 1988.

ISBN: 978-1-913955-00-7

FOR

Salud

'Every book you open, opens your mind.'

Spanish proverb

CONTENTS

MOSAICS OF SPAIN
SERIES INTRODUCTION

'*La experiencia, madre de las ciencias.*'
Experience, the mother of all knowledge.

Cervantes, *Don Quixote*

Over the course of more than twenty years writing about Spain, the most common question asked of me has always been, 'Why?' Why the continuing fascination with the country?

It's one of those deceptively simple queries which not only assumes that it has an answer, but also implies that this should be as equally straight-forward as itself.

The truth, however, is that it is possibly the most difficult thing for me to clarify. Early on, I would say something vague about 'the people', or 'the food', or even, if I was really desperate, 'the weather'. And deep down I knew I was lying. Not that I didn't like any of this, but because I wasn't saying what I really felt. Which, in turn, was due to the fact that I didn't understand, and so couldn't express, what I really felt.

Later, as I got used to being asked the same thing, I started talking about 'some indefinable quality' about Spain, and said I was writing books about the country in order to answer the question myself. That seemed to work for a while, but still I knew that I was really only dodging it. True, the books were, to an extent, an exploration of the matter, a way of trying to explain to myself my profound love of, and interest in, everything Spanish – a passion which had first begun when I was a teenager. But it was still no answer.

So, I began to think, perhaps there was no answer. This felt quite good. Accepting that possibility in itself was a liberation of sorts: I no longer felt obliged to come up with some excuse. I was simply fascinated with Spain. There was no 'why'.

And so, for a while, I stopped looking. My interest didn't wane, but I merely let it exist, let it take its own course, refrained from asking it to explain itself and tell me how and why it existed in the first place.

It was then that I began to realise that alongside this first question, I had been dogged by a second, which was equally hard to answer: *What* was Spain?

This is something which the Spanish themselves have been trying to answer since the very beginning, and it has dragged them into multiple civil wars and conflicts as they thrash out different possible solutions – a topic which I cover in my book *Violencia: A New History of Spain*. The problem is that 'Spain' is something immediately recognisable, and yet try defining it and you quickly get into trouble. Over many years the same experience has happened to me time and again: no sooner do I think 'Aha! Yes, *this* is Spain,' than its complete opposite rears its head and insists that *it* is as Spanish as my first observation. Hence a nation that can be equally colourful, and dour and austere; as cruel as it is compassionate and kind; as green and lush as it is dry and desert-like; as ingenious and forward-thinking as it is backward and conservative. Spain, I realised, resembled a chess-board, being simultaneously both black and white.

And yet, as earlier with the question of 'why?', I continued my search for the 'what?', an elusive essence, like a chest of buried treasure in a folk tale, which would somehow sum everything up. It was like being one of those scientists who try to find an equation which can explain absolutely everything in the Universe. I explored all manner of aspects of Spain, its history and culture, its food, its people and its creations. Many of these lines of investigation turned into more books – both fiction and non-fiction, because at this level, a personal one, they serve the same purpose.

But then, one day, I stopped writing. A combination of factors meant that for a while I contemplated never writing another book – on Spain or anything else. My search for the essence, the 'what?', of the country, simply came to an end. Just as my quest to find the 'why?' behind my fascination with it had ended beforehand.

Which was when, after some time, I began to realise that the two questions – which had both been with me for so long – were actually the same. Subconsciously I had reasoned that if I could discover the elusive something which was Spain, then I would also answer, for myself at least, the burning question of why I had been so enthralled by the place since adolescence. 'Why?' had never gone away; it had simply disguised itself in the form of 'What?'

And it was in this space – created by simply ceasing to look for *an* answer, *any* answer – that answers began to reveal themselves. I saw that what I had been looking for had, in fact, been in front of me all along: the unifying essence of Spain lay in its very multiplicity. Its many parts – even those elements which seemingly competed against each other – together made up a whole, like a thousand individual pieces which, when correctly combined, form a complex, beautiful and sometimes troubling mosaic – not unlike some of the dizzying geometric designs on the walls of the Alcázar in Seville, or the Alhambra in Granada. Trying to work them out only seemed to lead into a labyrinth of angles and numbers and proportions – fascinating in itself and yet somehow missing the point. The thing was to see them as a whole, to allow them simply to exist. To experience them.

So it was with Spain herself.

And, as a result, I started writing again, and a new project came into being – this series, *Mosaics of Spain*. It is a personal collection examining some of the many facets that make up what we know of as 'Spain'. It is, theoretically, endless, because I could spend several lifetimes exploring the country and its culture and still find new gems and treasures to share. But I only have this one lifetime, and so have focussed on the manifestations of Spain which have most spoken to me.

All the books are made up of new materials – both written and in some cases photographic – while also containing various articles I have scribbled for newspapers and magazines around the world, an assortment of essays, notes and stories, and selected passages from previously published books.

As Spain herself is a mosaic, so the series reflects this by being one in turn, while also acting as a mirror to the multiple Spanish subjects that I have covered in my previous books. Taken as a whole – and almost certainly combined with future books – they form a unified image: the mosaic of my own personal Spain, and what the country has meant to me.

My hope is that within this expression, others will find a resonance with their own experiences of the country – both ones in the past and those which are yet to come.

PREFACE
THE WORLD OF MAX CÁMARA

Valencia entered my life the day I met the woman who would later become my wife and the mother of our two children. My first encounter with Salud was in north Oxford, of all places (which is another story), but she hailed from Valencia and, as soon as I could, I flew over to visit her in her home town. Our first kiss was on the Cabanyal beach, not far from *La Pepica* paella restaurant, where she had taken me to sample 'the real thing', just how they make it in the city where it was first created.

Before too long, I was living in Valencia full time. When not writing, I was out exploring and taking pleasure in the warmth and easy friendliness of the people. It was not my first spell in Spain: in my mid-twenties I had spent three years in the country, moving from place to place. Valencia was not somewhere I had really got to know; in fact I had avoided it, largely on the advice of Spanish friends, who never spoke highly of the city. Yet now I had the chance to explore it myself, I realised how wrong they had been.

It was 1999, and Valencia had yet to be 'discovered' by outsiders. Many buildings in the older parts were run-down; whole blocks, in some places, lay in piles of rubble, untouched since some previous, largely forgotten, disaster. Graffiti – so much more prevalent in Spain than any other European country I knew – was scrawled on every available patch of wall. Walking the streets, blond, pale-skinned and over six feet tall, I was clearly an anomaly: heads frequently turned to see this strange, unfamiliar creature. It was a far cry from other parts of Spain, where almost half a century had passed since the sight of 'foreigners' had raised eyebrows.

I loved the city. Its fiestas – particularly the deafening, colour-filled rite of spring traditions surrounding Fallas – were fiery, orgiastic and frankly dangerous. It felt edgy and real, a place known only to locals, with strong traditions, a sense of its own unique identity, some of the best food I had ever tasted, and a playfulness that insisted there was only ever 'today': leave tomorrow's thoughts till well after dawn. And it was cheap. It was the perfect venue for a young couple in love experiencing their first intense years together.

The past two decades have seen great change in the city, however. Boom years came, heralded by the arrival of the Americas' Cup, Formula One racing, a visit by the Pope and a host of other international events. Money – huge amounts of it – seemed to fall from the sky like fairy dust: the crumbling old buildings got tarted up, new ones, very flashy and modern, were built. And with it all came a stench of corruption so foul you could smell it the moment you stepped out on to the street.

Then came the crash of 2008, and the money dried up – just as quickly as it had arrived. People were losing their jobs, joining queues at the food bank, throwing themselves from buildings. And the first stories about how much cash had lined the pockets of local politicians and businessmen started to go public.

It was at exactly this time that our first child was born. I had written four books by that point, ones which largely involved me travelling or being away for the purposes of research. Now we had a baby: I wanted to be at home more.

And so I started on a project that had been in the back of my mind for some time: a series of detective novels set in Valencia. I had avoided writing about the city until then, perhaps because I wanted it to seep in, to make sure that when I did it would come from some deeper level of knowledge and experience. But of course, if I was going to write detective novels, I was going to need a detective. Which was when Max Cámara appeared before me, fully formed, as though he'd simply been waiting for me all that time.

In the subsequent years, he has been the protagonist of six novels and one short story. Alongside, other key characters have joined him: Hilario, his anarchist-philosopher grandfather; Torres, his sarcastic fellow detective and friend; and Alicia, his lover and partner. The four of them have, as you might expect in a series of crime novels, gone through some ups and downs. But that is the nature not only of fictional characters, but real people as well, as events around the world at the time of writing only confirm. Fate often has surprises waiting for us around the corner, as Max himself knows only too well.

In the sixth novel, *Fatal Sunset*, Max came to what is technically called a sticky end. Or appeared to. Several correspondents wrote, quite distraught in some cases, asking if that was the end of my paella-loving detective. I hope that what they find at the end of this book – *An Interview with Max Cámara* – will set their minds at rest.

As for the other contents presented here, they are best seen as both part of the *Mosaics of Spain* series as well as a companion to the detective novels. There are articles on Valencia, potted histories of some of the most celebrated cases from the annals of Spanish True Crime, a master-class on Setting and Atmosphere for crime writers, a photographic essay on 'the Valencia of Max Cámara', a meeting with 'the Real Max Cámara' and lots more. For those who have been missing Max over the past few years, I hope it will go some way to filling the gap.

And, lastly, I should add that this book marks a new beginning. I have a strong feeling that Max's detecting services will be required again in the not-too-distant future.

Jason Webster

MAX CÁMARA

MAX CÁMARA

Chief Inspector Max Cámara of the Spanish National Police shuffled on his stool. He was in a grubby bar down a side alley at the back of the Valencia bullring, surrounded by bullfighting aficionados. He couldn't leave – not yet; protocol demanded he stay a few more minutes. And so he reverted to doing what he did best: watching, observing, recording – just like the 'camera' of his name.

A couple of metres away, the owner of the *Bar Los Toros* was chatting to his employee, busy pouring him another glass of red wine; the two men had to lean in to each other to hear themselves above the noise of the TV set bolted high in a corner, and a dozen other conversations bouncing off the red-painted greasy walls. The man they were all waiting for, Jorge Blanco, the star matador of the afternoon, still hadn't shown up. Worried expressions were becoming visible on the faces of the two dozen others crammed in the bar with him. So far, he had barely conversed with any of them: something about the chief inspector, his clothes, the cut of his hair, the lack of precision in his shaving, told them he wasn't one of them. And their body language said everything.

If anyone present had focussed on him at all, they would probably have described Cámara as an unassuming man, with short, dark, slightly ruffled hair crowning a high forehead, a larger than average chin, dark brown eyes and a crooked, fleshy nose – the kind or person who no doubt could look after himself, and had possibly done so on more than one occasion. More percep-tive observers of the forty-two-year-old might notice other details: strong yet thoughtful hands devoid of any rings, bracelets or watch; an observant expression in his lively brown eyes; and a vulnerability only partially masked by his broad shoulders and powerful physical presence. He was a man you would pass without a second glance down a street in broad daylight, but who might cause you some unease were the same situation repeated at night.

Sitting at the edge of the group, wondering whether to make a last attempt to talk to some of the other guests, a proverb – one of the dozens his grandfather used to repeat – floated through his mind: *Más vale estar solo que mal acompañado* – 'Better to be alone than in bad company.' He shouldn't have come.

The last mouthful of beer disappeared from his glass and he looked around the room. The other guests all looked to be *pijos* – rich, well-dressed conservatives: people he might have to mix with at work on occasion, but rarely chose to spend his free time with. The other side of Spain, the other tribe. He tapped his fingers on the bar. Five more minutes and then he'd go…

VALENCIA

MY VALENCIA

Fate and Love took me to Valencia; without them I'm not sure if I would ever have settled here, so bad was its reputation. But that was over ten years ago, and the place was very different then.

Only in recent years has this Mediterranean city – the third largest in Spain after Madrid and Barcelona – emerged from an ugly-duckling image it has endured for decades. Back in 1970, theatre critic Kenneth Tynan dubbed it 'the world capital of anti-tourism', revelling in its griminess, perverseness and lack of attention to the needs of visitors.

'To be alone in Valencia,' he quoted Lady Harlech as saying, 'is to be permanently twenty minutes this side of suicide.'

Punished by Franco for being the capital of the Republic during the Spanish Civil War, and unloved by much of the rest of the country, Valencia was a backwater, a jewel so encrusted with dirt that almost no one could see the treasure that was lying underneath – least of all the Valencians themselves.

But all that has changed. As I write, the very first high-speed trains are arriving in the city from Madrid, transporting passengers from the capital – over 350 kilometres away – in barely an hour and a half.

Yet this is only the latest in a long string of recent developments that have transformed Valencia into the most exciting city in Spain. Madrid may be the centre of power, and Barcelona a cultural hub, but Valencia offers the light and vibrancy of a major Mediterranean port, without the stress of an over-sized metropolis.

Perhaps the most emblematic symbol of the new Valencia is the City of

Arts and Sciences – a vast space-age complex of buildings designed by Valencian wunderkind Santiago Calatrava, one of the most fêted architects today. An opera house, a science museum, aquarium and showcase tennis court have all been constructed, attracting visitors from around the world, and are frequently used as the backdrop in adverts for new sports cars.

The attractions of the older part of the city have also been given some much-needed attention. When I first arrived, chunks of the Moorish city walls and wonderful 19th-century town houses were close to falling down. Valencia felt neglected and down-at-heel. Now, however, a great number of these buildings have been restored and painted, their facades shining bright pinks, reds and blues.

For this is a city that loves colour, pageantry and show, in all its forms. *Fallas*, the biggest fiesta of the year here – and one of the most important in the country – heralds the coming of spring. And Valencians like to mark the changing of the seasons with a concentration of fireworks, 'fire-cracker concerts' and bonfires that would pull at the heart strings of any self-respecting arsonist. Tonne after tonne of gunpowder is ignited in a seemingly endless display of pyrotechnics, both during the day and at night. While on the last day of the festivities, eight-metre-high statues of wood and papier-mâché, standing at almost every crossroads, are set ablaze, often scorching nearby buildings – and anyone foolish enough to stand too close.

There's more to the city than a strong pyromaniac tendency, though. Valencia is the home of Spain's national dish – paella. Here, the real thing is made with chicken and rabbit, not seafood – although there are fish and shellfish versions. But with the sea close by, and surrounded by a belt of fertile market gardens growing everything from oranges and artichokes to spinach and olives, this is an ideal place to test for oneself the health-giving benefits of the famous 'Mediterranean diet'.

Yet despite all this abundance and renewal, all is not rosy in Valencia. There is a dark side to the city, one that rarely comes to light or is seen by the visitor. Which was one of the reasons why I decided to write a series of detective novels set here. Having set down my roots over ten years before, I wanted to describe the place that had become my home, but to do so in a way that expressed the nuances, the shadows and tones of grey as well as all the colour and the attractions. Today no one could insist that this is a capital of 'anti-tourism', but the dirty, edgy city that Tynan saw hasn't gone away, not entirely.

Accusations of corruption among the city's political elite are so common now they barely warrant front-page attention. All that money that was used to help revamp the place was also used to line a few pockets, it would appear.

Then some of the decisions made in the name of progress have been very controversial. The Cabanyal is an old fishermen's quarter north of the port area, running parallel to the beach. Here tightly packed houses from the turn of the century display facades of delicate ceramic work, with blue, green and turquoise zigzag patterns or checkerboard effects, with decorations showing sea creatures or the faces of water spirits. The area has been described by more than one visitor as an 'open-air museum', a showcase of Art Nouveau design. Yet the Town Hall wants to bulldoze a great hole through the neighbourhood to extend a modern avenue to the seafront. Local people have staged protests, and there have been clashes with the police, but the plans continue.

And of course, as with almost any modern city, Valencia has its own fair share of problems with drugs and the sex trade. In fact, the city had an official red-light district as far back as the Middle Ages. And as you drive along the local roads today you will often find a lonely building somewhere, the word 'club' in fluorescent lights over the door. Don't be fooled: this is not the local equivalent of White's or the Athenaeum, but a brothel.

Despite its faults, though, I have developed a deep attachment to Valencia. I came originally because I had fallen in love with a Valencian woman; today she is my wife. And although, in that sense, the choice of where I was to come and live in Spain was made for me, I now know I would have it no other way. Valencia is, and will continue to be, a great Spanish city. And there is more than enough material here for many more crime novels to come.

This article first appeared in The Telegraph *in 2010*

MAX CÁMARA'S VALENCIA

Five minutes later, wearing a clean shirt, his hair still damp, Max Cámara set out to walk the ten minutes to Almudena's flat, on the other side of the Ruzafa quarter. Lying just to the south of the old centre, the neighbourhood was no longer the refuge of drug dealers it had once been; now Moroccan grocery shops sat next to Chinese wholesalers of cheaply made clothes, and antique dealers selling Art Deco furniture. Cámara liked it for its friendly, village atmosphere.

Architecturally, as with much of Valencia, it was a mixture of elegant, brightly painted Eclectic apartment blocks – five or six storeys high, with tall narrow French windows and ornate iron railings – standing next to younger, more awkward siblings: ugly, brown-brick structures from the 1950s and 1960s, with bright orange awnings and aluminium doors. The Carmen area a twenty-minute walk away – the oldest quarter, near the cathedral – managed to retain a more historic feel. There the streets were narrower, windier and dirtier, giving a sense of the labyrinthine atmosphere of the medieval city, and a feeling of intimacy – in a relatively small city like this it was common to bump into friends and acquaintances.

Among the graffitied walls and abandoned houses with weeds growing out of their crumbling roofs, some of the more important buildings, like the late-Gothic *Lonja* silk exchange with its spiralling pillars and lustful gargoyles, and the *Generalitat* palace, with delicate needle-column windows and large fan-like stone arches over the main doors, were a reminder that five hundred years before, Valencia had been the richest and most important city in Spain, home to the Borgias – before they became Popes and moved to Rome – and power-house of the Spanish Renaissance.

Fallas, the biggest fiesta in the city's year, was just beginning and some of the roads had already been cleared of parked cars for the garish statues that the next day would be erected at every crossroads. The *Falleros* – those Valen-cians actively involved in the fiesta – always took over the city for a fortnight like an army of occupation. And this year – as every year, it seemed – the authorities were boasting of a million visitors expected from abroad and other parts of Spain. When it came to Fallas, there was a clear division in the city between those who loved it and those who didn't and who left town to get away from the all-encompassing noise. Cámara had long counted himself among the anti-fallero group.

Three boys no older than seven were huddled outside the doorway as Cámara headed down the stairs to the front door of his block of flats. Through the glass he could see the dark red glow of the fuse for the firecracker as it snaked along the paving stones towards its target. The boys stood up and scattered, and a second later the inevitable BANG of the explosive filled the street. Get it wrong and some *petardos* could take a finger off. But Valencian boys were brought up with this, as though they learnt the Dos and Don'ts through some kind of osmosis. Moments later they were back in position, another firecracker – a powerful *trueno* this time – ready to light. This would go on all day, and there were tens of thousands of similar groups all over the city, all with an uncontrollable greed for noise.

After today there were only three working days left, then the real holidays started and the hard-core pyromaniac fun could begin.

The walk to work took him down streets lined with palm trees and acacias until he connected with the old river which led him up to the brand new police *Jefatura*. The Turia had once flowed this way, a tiny little stream snaking down a wide, empty river bed. Every once in a while it had filled with the flood waters from the inland mountains and had become a proper river for a few short days or weeks before returning to is habitual trickle. But then, in 1957, it broke even these copious banks, and the city had found itself three metres under water. So they had diverted the whole thing around to the south of the city, and the old river bed had been turned into a park, an arching streak of green through a densely packed city. Thank God they had made the right choice in the end – at one stage Franco had wanted to turn it into a six-lane ring-road.

A clear spring sky shone overhead as Cámara neared the gleaming white of his new offices. What had been intended as an art museum for the city had been converted at the last minute into a police station when the banks pulled the plug on the Town Hall's massive debts. The architectural masterpiece by Valencian wunderkind Jaume Montesa, designed to crown the transformation of the city from provincial backwater to Mediterranean powerhouse, was now struggling to function as the hub of police activity for the whole region. Practical considerations like places to park hadn't been at the forefront of the great man's mind, more concerned with the lines of his parallel white cement arches, and the blue crystal walls that were meant to reflect the waters of the sea just a couple of miles to the east.

Cámara caught the now-familiar smell of stale urine floating in from the side of the main entrance where colleagues unwilling to climb the stairs or take the lift to the only toilet, on the fourth floor, relieved themselves after enjoying a couple of cigarettes away from their smoke-free offices. Groups of them were standing around as he approached, some in uniform, the *judiciales* like himself in ordinary clothes. As part of *Homicidios* Cámara was regarded by some colleagues as being near the top of the tree – where they all wanted to be if they'd admit it. And now he'd just landed himself the murder of the century. A couple of them nodded as he walked past. Maldonado was there as well, but pretended to look the other way…

FIESTA

FALLAS

'Careful. Those firecrackers can take a finger off.'

Vicente, my neighbour, isn't joking. As I place the offending petard back in its box, he raises a hand to show a missing section on the middle digit of his right hand.

'Happened years ago,' he says with a shrug. 'When I was a kid.'

Valencia, in March. The mercury is rising, the sun beats down; spring is in the air. While the vernal equinox is celebrated elsewhere with a quiet stroll and a picnic in the countryside, here on Spain's Mediterranean coast, after eleven months of relative restraint, Valencians are once again indulging their greatest passion: letting off vast quantities of colourful, dangerous and very loud fireworks.

There is something almost heart-warming in these overly cautious times to discover that in one corner of Europe, for a few weeks of the year at least, seven-year-old boys are walking the streets with boxes of explosives under their arms, scorching their fingertips as they fiddle with fuses in the middle of the pavement. Forget health-and-safety: fire and noise – so loud it can make your ears bleed – are the watchwords for one of the most spectacular fiestas in Spain.

I've been living in Valencia now for ten years, married to a local girl – a flamenco dancer – my two sons both born here. And Fallas has become a part of my life. Like most Valencian families, we tend to measure the year in terms of 'before' and 'after' Fallas, as others might do with Christmas.

For Fallas is more than a celebration of springtime. Perhaps more than any other Spanish fiesta, it has come to define this city – its mindset, its way of doing things. For some, it is an indication of the playful, energetic spirit of Valencians. For critics, it represents a tacky frivolity and lack of substance.

A *falla*, after which the fiesta takes its name (from the Latin *facula*, 'torch'), is a brightly painted and often gaudy statue made of wood, foam and wax which can stand anywhere between one and thirty metres high. It usually comprises a number of figures – *ninots* – often satirical in character, which may represent real people (politicians and celebrities), concepts ('the sea', 'fame'), or pretty much anything that was passing though the sculptor's mind at the time. Having been constructed over the previous year in a suburb known as *La Ciudad Fallera*, hundreds of these statues are erected all over the city at crossroads and in squares during the early part of March. For weeks, streets are closed, parties are held in the open air, and firecrackers are let off in abundance, while large-scale firework displays light up the night sky. Then, on 19 March, St Joseph's Day, at around midnight the *fallas* are ceremoniously burnt down, almost simultaneously, in a bacchanalian frenzy as enormous crowds surge around the flames, intoxicated by a curious primal energy. 'Orgy of fire' doesn't even come close.

St Joseph is the patron saint of carpenters, which gives weight to the theory that Fallas started with a local carpenters' tradition of burning poles or planks of wood used for suspending candles during the dark winter months, and which were no longer needed with the coming of spring. Others talk of a legacy from the Middle Ages, when artisans cleared out their workshops as the days grew longer, burning what they no longer needed. Whatever the origin, insisting this essentially pagan celebration of the equinox has anything to do with St Joseph or Christian rites doesn't really stick: there is none of the heavy seriousness of the Easter processions here. Indeed, the Christian calendar events that fall on either side of it – Lent and Easter – have all but vanished from the city, so imposing and dominating has it become. Fallas is all about the changing of the season, and having fun, whether you want to or not.

The official dates of the festival are 15-19 March, but few pay attention to that and each year it seems to start earlier. Certainly by the second week in March the party is well underway.

A typical Fallas day goes something like this:

Having just managed to get to sleep after the revelry of the night before, you are woken up at eight o'clock sharp by the *Despertà* – a brass band walking the streets playing very loud *pasodobles*. Any thoughts of catching a few more minutes between the sheets are soon abandoned as what sounds like a fierce gun battle quickly breaks out beneath your bedroom window. Those are not AK-47s firing off, however, but local children innocently throwing potent firecrackers at each other, as they will continue to do so for the remainder of the day and well into the night. Silence is a rare and precious commodity during Fallas. If you crave it, do as thousands of non-*fallero* Valencians and leave town as fast as you can.

Stumbling bleary-eyed out on to the street, your body's cry for high doses of sugar to kick-start you into action are catered for by dozens of fried-food stalls. Here you can get Spanish-style hot chocolate, so thick you could plaster walls with it, and *buñuelos*, the main Fallas delicacy, made of battered pieces of pumpkin dough. Get them freshly made and they are delicious.

With your stomach duly lined, the rest of the morning involves *pasacalles* – small-scale processions where more traditional music is played. This is an opportunity for locals to show off their special Fallas costumes. Made at great expense in embroidered silk – once a major Valencian export – these stylised 18th-century dresses are paraded with great pomp, the women braiding their hair into flat discs at the sides of their heads in traditional style (not unlike the coils on the Iberian *Lady of Elche* statue).

By now it's past one o'clock, and you notice that many people are starting to leave, all walking in the same direction. Following them, you come out into the *Plaza del Ayuntamiento*, a large square in the centre of the city. This is the setting for one of the most important daily Fallas rituals – the *Mascletà*.

'A concert of fire-crackers' might be the best way to describe this. Others might use terms like 'a lot of banging', or 'sheer lunacy'. With tens of thousands of people tightly packed around a fenced-off area in the middle of the square, on the dot of two, thousands of fireworks and firecrackers are ignited, creating a barrage of noise that well exceeds 120 decibels. Revellers stand watching open-mouthed, not in awe but because they know that to close your mouth risks blowing your ear-drums, so powerful is the sound. Red Cross ambulances are on standby for anyone foolish enough not to follow their example.

The effect of attending a *Mascletà* is interesting. Personally, it is the only time when I've had the impression of actually *seeing* sound, like some special-effect wave in a sci-fi movie. That's apart from feeling the explosions reverberate through parts of my body I didn't know existed. Then there's the light-headed feeling that comes when it finishes (it usually lasts about seven to ten minutes). Well, that's because the banging has finally ended, you might think. But curiously you can feel quite cleansed afterwards, and a spontaneous camaraderie will develop with strangers standing nearby, as though you have shared something significant by witnessing this powerful event together.

With the *Mascletà* over, it's time for lunch, which can mean only one thing in Valencia – paella. As the home of what has become Spain's national dish, be prepared to taste the real thing, made with chicken, rabbit and beans. Some of it might be cooked over open fires built in the middle of the road, other servings can be found in bars and restaurants dotted about the city.

Sleep of any kind is officially frowned on during Fallas, but some might try to put their heads down for a quick siesta before the afternoon's activities. For bullfight enthusiasts, Valencia hosts one of the most important early events of the season, with many big names appearing. Others might stroll the streets, admiring the *fallas*. Meanwhile the *falleros* make another appearance in their traditional costumes, this time moving in slow procession carrying bunches of carnations to take to the *Plaza de la Virgen* next to the cathedral, where a large floral statue of the Virgin is built as the 'offerings' are brought in.

By nightfall it is time for more firework displays, the largest being on 18 March – the *Nit de Foc*, the 'Night of Fire'. Then on 19 March comes the culmination of the entire fiesta – the *Cremà*, when the *fallas* are finally burnt down. Firemen stand ready, dowsing nearby buildings with water to prevent them from spontaneously combusting. The crowds stand and watch, hypnotised by the flames, as sparks and plumes of thick black smoke surge into the night air.

With ears ringing from the explosions, nerves shattered from lack of sleep, the smell of acrid smoke permeating your clothes, you eventually fall exhausted back into bed, sound in the knowledge that you have lived through one of the most insane fiestas on the planet, and survived.

And for the first time in what feels like an eternity, as you place your head on the pillow, you listen and hear… nothing.

This article first appeared in the FT Travel *section in 2011*

SPANISH TRUE CRIME CASE NO. 1

THE WEREWOLF OF GALICIA

THE WEREWOLF OF GALICIA

Spain's first recorded serial killer was born in the north-western region of Galicia in 1809. Manuel Blanco Romasanta's parents thought their child was a girl for the first six years of his life, for which reason he was baptised as 'Manuela'. Only after a doctor examined him was the mistake realised and his name changed to Manuel.

Manuel lived a relatively comfortable life and learnt how to read and write – an uncommon thing in 19th-century rural Spain. He grew up to be a small man, measuring less than five feet, with blond hair and what were described as 'tender' features. He married, but was soon widowed, and became a travelling salesman working across Galicia and northern Portugal.

In 1844 Romasanta was accused of killing an official who had tried to collect debts of 600 reales which he owed to a supplier in Ponferrada. Romasanta fled capture, was tried in his absence and sentenced to ten years in prison.

After living in hiding for over a year, he reappeared under a false name, pretending to be Portuguese, in the small village of Rebordachao, not far from his place of birth. Soon he made friends with a local woman named Manuela, who had recently separated from her husband and was looking for work. Romasanta convinced Manuela that he had friends in the coastal city of Santander who needed a maid: he could take her there himself and secure her the job. Manuela agreed and the two set off. Some time later Romasanta returned to the village, informing Manuela's family that all was well and that she was now secure in her new position. Not only that, but they also had a position for Manuela's sister, Benita. Benita agreed to go and, accompanied by her ten-year-old son, headed off with Romasanta for the coast. In the months that followed, two other women from the village left their homes and were taken by Romasanta with the promise of work, each time taking their children with them.

Time passed, however, and back in the village the families of the women who had left began to find it strange that they had not received any word from their loved ones. Romasanta tried forging letters from them, but sensing that his luck was running out, he fled.

It was then that he made a crucial mistake: he tried to sell clothes belonging to the missing women. The authorities found out, caught up with him, and he was arrested.

It was 1853. Romasanta confessed to the murder of nine people in cold blood, adding that he had practised cannibalism on his victims. Not only that, he had also taken fats from their bodies with which he had made soap, selling his wares as he travelled the countryside. In defence of his actions, however, he gave a curious explanation: he claimed that he was not responsible as a spell had been cast on him which turned him into a wolf. Episodes in this wolverine state lasted anything up to eight days. The court was intrigued, but when asked to turn himself into a wolf – in order to demonstrate his claim – Romasanta refused: it was impossible, he said, as the spell only lasted thirteen years and had ended just the week before.

The judge found him guilty and condemned him to be garrotted to death.

But that was not the end of the story. In London, a French hypnotist had been following the trial of the Spanish wolfman, which was avidly reported in the international press. This man went under the name of 'Mr Philips' but was possibly the French physician Joseph-Pierre Durand de Gros, whose writings would later inspire Freud and Jung's thinking on the workings of the mind. 'Philips' now wrote to the Spanish government asking to be given a chance to cure Romasanta, claiming that he had a track record in such cases of 'clinical lycanthropy' – in which a person believes themselves to be a werewolf. The Spanish Minister of Justice heard about the Frenchman's interest and himself appealed to Queen Isabella to commute Romasanta's sentence to life imprisonment. The monarch agreed.

Unfortunately, it is here that the trail of the story goes cold, and what exactly happened to Romasanta next is unclear. He was spared the garrotte, but no details have survived of what happened between him and the hypnotist. Was he ever 'cured'? No one can say. For a long time it was thought that Romasanta died shortly after starting his sentence in the prison of Celanova.

Recent research, however suggests that he died of stomach cancer in a prison in Ceuta in 1863, ten years after his trial.

Nonetheless, his name lives on: at least three novels and two films have been inspired by his bloody, and wolf-inspired, exploits.

DETECTIVE FICTION,
AUTHORITY &
SUBVERSION

THE DETECTIVE AS 'PRIEST'

To judge a society Dostoevsky suggested looking at its prisons, Gandhi at how it treats its weakest members. Others have put forward different criteria, but the culture of a particular country would appear an obvious place to begin. The artwork, literature and music its people create tell us an enormous amount about their values – in a very general sense.

If we wanted to draw more specific conclusions about a society, however, its novels and paintings give some details and a broad brush-stroke idea of a particular time and place. But the images they portray can be subjective and act like single pieces of a complex jigsaw puzzle that can never be completed.

Yet the mere existence or not of one particular literary genre tells us much about a specific aspect of a society's makeup: its relationship with authority, be it spiritual or temporal. How much power an officially sanctioned belief system holds can be gauged by a country's production – or lack of – detective fiction.

Clearly, censorship of any kind puts limitations on most artistic endeavours. Yet the arts have always survived, not least crime fiction, which is one of the oldest literary genres in existence: we only have to look at the Bible and the story of Cain and Abel to see what a long pedigree it has. And its popularity has remained virtually undiminished for centuries.

Detective fiction, however, is different. Stories where a crime is committed and then – usually – an individual follows leads, finds clues and eventually solves the mystery, only emerge in societies in which the official creeds are under threat or actually crumbling. And in cases where, after a revolutionary change, one form of authoritarianism is replaced by another, detective fiction often blossoms quite briefly only to be smothered – or, in one interesting example, appropriated – by the incoming regime.

The pattern becomes apparent when one takes a look at the history and development of detective fiction. There are differing opinions about when it actually began: the first modern detective novel is usually attributed either to William Godwin's *Caleb Williams*, published in 1794, or to Edgar Allen Poe's *The Murders in the Rue Morgue*, which came out in 1841.

What few argue, however, is that the 1860s witnessed the birth of the genre of detection fiction as a whole. This was the decade that saw the publication of Wilkie Collins's *The Moonstone*, which was, in the opinion of C S Lewis, 'the first, the longest and the best modern English detective novel.'

Britain was not the only country enjoying this new kind of writing. In France, Emile Gaboriou published his first *roman judiciaire* in 1866. *L'Affaire Lerouge* was a big success and spawned a series of novels involving the amateur detective Monsieur Lecoq.

Theories explaining the successful birth of detective fiction at this time have tended to focus on developments in society in the mid 19th century. Industrialisation and the growth of literacy meant that more people were able to read than before. Machinery was developed that could satisfy this new market, producing cheap books in vast numbers. In Britain, W H Smith took advantage of the burgeoning reading public by setting up stalls in railway stations where passengers could easily buy something to help pass the time on their journeys. His bestsellers were often sensational stories that literary types sneered at.

'Tawdry novels which flare in the bookshelves of our railway stations, and which seem designed, as so much else that is produced for the use of our middle class, for people with a low standard of life,' Matthew Arnold complained.

Unabashed, ordinary readers were eager for ever more of this kind of stuff, and when the first detective novels came along they were lapped up.

Of course, detective fiction could not have come about had it not been for the creation of the 'detective' itself. This had occurred in 1842, when the Metropolitan Police created its 'Detective Branch'. The first such policeman who came to wide public notice was Jack Whicher, called in to investigate the Road Hill House murder in Wiltshire in 1860. The case was followed avidly by newspapers describing every twist and development. Soon there was barely a person in the country who did not have a theory about who had murdered Francis Kent.

All these elements were undoubtedly important in the rise of detective fiction in the 1860s. But what accounted for the sudden fascination with the figure of the detective? Why did detective stories become such huge best sellers almost overnight at this particular time? And how has a genre that was – and still is – viewed as inferior managed to survive so long?

An answer can be found by thinking about what a detective actually does. He or she is essentially an answer-giver, a problem-solver, someone who can restore order where there is chaos. Faced with the worst crime – and what could be more existential than a murder? – the detective gives us solutions to the pressing and urgent question, Whodunnit? And he does so by taking us on a journey, discovering pieces of evidence, seeking out hints and clues. In the nature of the game, the reader, too, sees what he sees, is shown the same things, but is unable to solve the crime. Only the detective, in a final display of mastery and superior ability, is capable of interpreting the clues to reach the correct conclusion. We need him, and his special knowledge and abilities, to make sense of it all.

Structurally, then, a detective is similar to a priest. It has been a prerequisite of the clerical castes that have existed throughout history to claim a capacity to solve important, existential problems. In many religious or sacred traditions it was precisely the priest's role to give official answers to the great questions of life as ordinary people were not considered fit to reach their own conclusions. (And heaven forbid that they should reach conclusions that went against the status quo.)

Seen in this way, a development almost simultaneous with the explosion of detective fiction in Britain and France around the 1860s helps explain the birth of the literary genre and its immediate popularity.

Darwin published *On the Origin of Species* on 24 November 1859. The theory of evolution did not come in a vacuum and many were already moving away from the literal interpretation of the Bible's Creation stories before Darwin's ideas went public. But the fact that we still commemorate his work is testament to the importance that it has played in the forging of the modern Western world. Perhaps no other single event played such an important part in the shift from a religious to a secular society. In other words, no other event did so much to undermine the power and authority of clerics and their officially sanctioned answers and solutions to questions of existence.

The world did not become secular overnight, but the bubble had been burst: representatives of the church could no longer claim a monopoly on truth.

It is no coincidence that just as this group of answer-givers was being undermined that another kind of answer-giver was rising so prominently. Religious men and women and the ideas they represented had been seriously challenged, but they also played an important and necessary role – that of someone who ordinary people could turn to with important questions. Now someone else had to fulfil that function. And in a changing world, where new dangers and problems were appearing, into the breach stepped the fictional detective.

He did not claim to have specific answers to questions about the meaning or origins of existence, but he did solve problems, he did, when faced with the taking of life, bring about a resolution and made the world a better place again – no matter how temporarily. On a symbolic level he played the role of the cleric that the industrial and now increasingly secular world had deposed.

Examine in this way the greatest fictional detective of all – Sherlock Holmes – and the parallels become clear. Holmes is – probably – celibate. He acts in the ordinary world, but his natural habitat, his home, is a strange and exotic place where he often remains in isolation for weeks before emerging with answers and insights that can help solve the problems of those around him. Despite standing in Central London, 221B Baker Street has an other-worldliness about it that echoes a monastery or mystical retreat. Holmes resembles a Franciscan, periodically leaving his friary to move among the wider community and offer wisdom. Or a shaman, locked in his refuge, taking powerful drugs and communing with spirits before returning to ordinary life with mysterious powers and solutions.

"A Scandal in Bohemia" is an interesting example of his shamanic/priestly nature. At the beginning, living alone after Dr Watson's marriage, Holmes has been in his rooms for weeks 'buried among his old books' and taking cocaine. Upon the arrival of a Count Von Kramm, Holmes quickly demonstrates his superior powers of perception and understanding of human psychology by revealing that the count is actually the King of Bohemia. Later he disguises himself – as a clergyman no less – in order to discover the secrets of Irene Adler, who is suspected of blackmailing the king. With the threat of fire – symbolic of 'Hellfire' – she reveals where she is hiding a compromising photo of the monarch, thus solving the mystery. The twist in the tale is that Adler then tricks Holmes and vanishes with the photo. Watson declares that for Holmes she was always 'the woman' – the only one whom he ever really admired – but of course has no physical relationship with.

In a world which was losing faith in priests in general, it is no wonder that the almost superhuman and yet flawed Holmes became so popular. Nor is it surprising, perhaps, that his creator, should have had such a strong interest in the supernatural: in the latter part of his life, Sir Arthur Conan Doyle was an avid supporter of psychics and mediums.

Equally, it is notable that after Holmes one of the best loved fictional detectives is a priest. G K Chesterton's Father Brown is a quiet and bumbling character but he has un unfailing intuition that allows him to solve crimes that are beyond the capacities of mere policemen. Like Holmes, he often tricks criminals into revealing themselves – as a believer might confess his sins – by disguising his true character. In the "The Blue Cross" not only the master thief Flambeau but the Parisian detective chasing him across England, Valentin, are completely taken in by the 'moon-calf' appearance of the very short priest from Essex. Chesterton was a Catholic himself. By creating an investigating cleric, he may well have been trying to close the gap, to put the genie of secularisation back into the bottle and restore the priest to his former standing.

Other fictional sleuths betray a correlation between detective and cleric, often in their names. John Rhodes's forensic scientist Dr Priestley is an obvious example. The biblical associations of John Creasey's Commander George Gideon are clear, while other names with religious connotations are not uncommon, even for contemporary characters: Adrian Monk and John Luther have both been tremendous hits on television in recent years, while Michael Dibdin's Aurelio Zen, James Patterson's Alex Cross and Leslie Charteris's Simon Templar 'The Saint' are among the most celebrated detectives in the history of the genre.

The fictional detective is not simply a replacement for a deposed caste of clerics, however. He represents a challenge to any system that claims to offer all the answers. The response in many countries after organised religions lost their monopolies on belief was to turn to other forms of ideology and the creation of political or politicised 'priests'. It is interesting to note how, in almost all of these cases, detective fiction enjoyed a brief flourishing only to be snuffed out or strictly controlled by the new, post-religious regime.

In Russia, Dostoevsky and Chekhov had written crime fiction in the 19th century, but proper detective stories did not take off until after the 1917 revolution and the fall of the Tsar. The 'Pinkerton Phenomenon' of the 1920s saw millions of copies of pulp novels being sold, usually with swashbuckling, American-style heroes fighting international crime. The Soviet government was uneasy with the genre, however, and with the increase in state control over everyday life, Stalin banned it. The restrictions were not lifted until after he died.

Italy followed a similar pattern. In 1929 Mondadori started publishing *i libri gialli* – cheap detective novels with yellow covers, and they sold in huge numbers. As with Soviet totalitarianism, however, the Fascist state disapproved and banned the genre entirely in 1941.

True crime stories were very popular in Germany in the 19th century and a few writers experimented with crime fiction. The growth of detective fiction did not begin in earnest until after the end of World War I and the fall of the Kaiser. One of the most influential of the new detective writers was Erich Kästner, author of *Emil and the Detectives*. His books were burned by the Nazis when they came to power in 1933. Interestingly, however, the Nazis did not ban the detective genre outright. Instead they controlled it, outlawing foreign detective writers and ensuring that German *Krimis* – which were hugely popular – depicted honest and highly competent policemen upholding the rule of law. Thus it became a part of the Nazi propaganda machine, providing an image of a powerful and controlling state.

Spain bucks this trend slightly in that there was no early flourishing of detective fiction. Despite a brief period of liberalisation during the Second Republic of the 1930s, the Church did not begin to lose its grip on power until the latter days of Franco's strictly Catholic regime. In the 1960s, as the country slowly began to change, Francisco García Pavón started a series of novels based around his policeman, Plinio. The genre really came to life, however, with Manuel Vázquez Montalbán and his Pepe Carvalho series, the first of which came out in 1972, when the dictatorship was already being challenged and Spaniards were looking towards a new, democratic future.

Not all countries saw religious power replaced by a new all-encompassing political ideology. Britain is an obvious example, but the experience of the United States in this regard sheds a fascinating light on the relationship between detective fiction and authority.

Pulp detective novels, like those that appeared in the *Black Mask* magazine, were hugely popular in the States after World War I. Yet this was also the period of Prohibition, perhaps the single most obvious manifestation of religious power in the country. Dashiell Hammett published *The Maltese Falcon*, considered the first proper American detective novel, in 1930, three years before Prohibition came to an end. The genre came of age with Chandler's *The Big Sleep*, however, which did not come out until 1939.

The American relationship with detective fiction is certainly influenced by the cowboy, an indigenous character not dissimilar to the detective. But the rise of the American hard-boiled style marked a fundamental shift in the genre. Tired of the purely intellectual crossword style puzzling of the 'Golden Age' writers in Britain, Chandler and Hammett wanted to produce something grittier and darker.

Viewed through the detective-as-cleric lens, the extent of the change that characters like Phillip Marlowe introduced comes into clear focus. In *The Big Sleep*, several people are killed before we reach the conclusion of the mystery – Marlowe is quite ineffective at preventing further bloodshed. And the murderer of Rusty Regan, whose disappearance Marlowe was originally called in to solve, turns out to be his employer's daughter. In a story depicting a murky world of blackmail and homosexuality – then a scandalous subject – there are no clear 'good guys' and 'bad guys'. The hero kills people, while the murderer turns out to be insane and is sent to an asylum.

The usual structure of previous detective novels is followed – a crime is committed and by the end of the book it is resolved. Yet unlike Holmes or Poirot, the American detective does not come across as a 'master', as a person who can almost automatically provide the answers. He is not priest-like in that sense. He is not superhuman, or pure, or a member of a caste with privileged knowledge beyond the grasp of ordinary people. He is essentially one of us; he is just as ordinary and complex as the reader.

This was an enormous shift. The detective no longer provided solutions from a position of superiority. He was struggling to resolve crises – to solve mysteries – just like anyone else. He muddled through until, in the end, he found some kind of answer. And it was rarely the neat and final conclusion of Agatha Christie novels. More often than not loose ends were left untied, the crime was solved but the world remained as messy and difficult after as it was before.

It would take a country like the USA, perhaps, where no church had been officially tied to state power, to make this leap. The result, however, was to revivify a genre that was in danger of becoming a footnote of literary history.

The result has been that the detective has evolved and continues to change to this day. Turned into an everyman, he reflects the society in which he finds himself: the shift away from a symbolic priest means that his canvas has expanded almost indefinitely – in theory there could be as many fictional detectives now as there are individuals.

A character like Inspector Morse hints at the continued struggle with the enigma of existence (and an underlying message) and confines his search to the quasi-monastic world of Oxford, but more contemporary writers' choices for their detectives' names give clues as to the underlying preoccupations of our time. Jo Nesbo's Harry Hole, Mark Billingham's Tom Thorne and Arnaldur Indridason's Detective Erlendur (from the Icelandic, meaning 'Outsider') point to a sense of isolation and emptiness, a world where, perhaps, no meaning or answers can ever be found.

And the common targets of a contemporary detective's investigations – corrupt politicians, or crimes committed by entire institutions in some cases, as in the television series *The Wire* – show clearly where the threats to our society are to be found. In the beginning, the very existence of a fictional detective was a challenge to state ideology; today the characters continue to fight for a freer and more liberal world, if only by trying to expose the potentially constraining and restricting forces that surround us. The basic opponent of the detective is the criminal, but who the criminal is, what his intentions are and who he is associated with have a parallel symbolism of their own.

The continued and growing success of detective fiction confirms that, in the West at least, we are not living in an authoritarian world, despite the ever-present threats to our liberties and privacy. But it does more – it clearly demonstrates how far we have moved from a belief in ideology per se. Overarching theories of everything are viewed now with scepticism or perhaps nostalgia, but not taken seriously. We have gone beyond believing in belief, and the modern detective – cynical, world-weary, but stubborn, probing and intent on finding a resolution – reflects in many ways our own attempts to find answers about existence. Not through the mouth-pieces of social order, but by ourselves, as individuals, each finding his or her own way. Day by day. Murder by murder.

This article first appeared in Aeon *magazine in 2013*

SPANISH TRUE CRIME CASE NO. 2
THE CRIME THAT NEVER WAS

THE CRIME THAT NEVER WAS

Cuenca is a sleepy, inland, rural province in eastern Spain. Sparsely populated and with a landscape made up mostly of the high tablelands of the Spanish *Meseta*, very little takes place there… usually. It was here in 1910, however, that one of the most infamous miscarriages of justice in Spanish history took place, still remembered to this day as *El Crimen de Cuenca* – 'the Crime of Cuenca'. Years after the case was cleared up, it would be turned into a novel, and then decades later still into a film – which in turn would be censored by a nominally democratic State, so shocking and damaging was the story it told.

Everything began in the small village of Osa de la Vega, where lived a young shepherd named José María Grimaldos. Grimaldos was commonly known amongst his peers as *el Cepa* – 'the stump' – in light of his short stature and learning disabilities. He was often the butt of jokes amongst the other boys, but two in particular, León Sánchez and Gregorio Valero, were known to be especially keen on making fun of his height, and frequently bullied him. One day, Grimaldos was seen by other villagers walking out with these two youngsters along the road towards the nearby village of Tresjuncos. Sánchez and Valero later returned, but of Grimaldos there was no trace. He had simply vanished.

The alarm was raised. Searches were carried out, but no sign of the young man could be found. People began to fear the worst. Then Grimaldos's family, remembering the taunts their boy had received from Sánchez and Valero, and remembering that they had been the last people to see him, began to draw conclusions. They accused the pair of murder; they had, they said, killed him to rob him of money from the sale of a number of sheep.

The accusation was taken seriously. Sánchez and Valero were detained and a judge was appointed to investigate the case. But the following year, in 1911, he released them for lack of evidence.

Back in the village, however, tongues continued to wag. By 1913 a new judge had arrived and, at the insistence of the Grimaldos family, reopened the case.

The main suspects were detained once again. This time the authorities were determined to extract a confession from them. Sánchez and Valero were brutally tortured by Civil Guards, who beat them up, suspended them in the air by their genitals, and pulled out their nails, facial hair and teeth. Finally, unable to take any more, the two young men confessed. At first they said they had buried Grimaldos's body. When asked where, they claimed they had burnt it. Yet when no trace of it could be found, they changed their story again, saying they had chopped it up and fed it to the pigs.

Despite these discrepancies, and other obvious problems with their confession, Sánchez and Valero were finally convicted of murder and given sentences of eighteen years each. They only just managed to avoid the death penalty.

Twelve years later, in 1925, both men were let out prison on early release. They both returned home, but found a cold welcome back in the village. Branded by their neighbours as confessed murderers, they found it hard to find work or return to their normal lives.

But then, not long after, rumours started to circulate about sightings of Grimaldos, their supposed murder victim. These grew until eventually the priest of Tresjuncos received a request for Grimaldos's baptism certificate on the grounds that the man, now living in the town of Mira, about 150 kilometres away, needed it to get married. The priest didn't answer, thinking it was some kind of cruel joke. But a few weeks later, none other than Grimaldos himself showed up in the village in order to get the document. After identifying himself to the priest and the authorities, news quickly spread around the country that the victim in the Cuenca 'crime' was anything but dead, but had been alive and healthy all this time. The Justice Minister was informed, and in due course Sánchez and Valero were pardoned.

It became a notorious case of miscarriage of justice, and symbolic of the kind of brutal power often exercised in rural communities by the paramilitary Civil Guard police. The writer Ramon J Sender turned the story into a novel in 1939, and then in 1979 a film version was made. Franco had died four years before and in the newly democratic Spain there supposedly was no censorship.

But the Minister of Culture at the time, Ricardo de la Cierva (a historian who painted Franco and his regime in a favourable light) banned the film on the grounds that it was insulting to the police authorities. It took another judge to overturn his ruling, in 1981, and the film was finally shown in cinemas around the country. It quickly became the highest grossing release in Spanish history at the time.

A CRIME-WRITING MASTERCLASS

SETTING AND ATMOSPHERE

SETTING AND ATMOSPHERE

Atmosphere was what Simenon called 'the poetic line' of a book and it was his starting point for every novel, the mood into which he poured his characters and plot, the environment in which they developed.

If you are interested in atmosphere in crime novels, study Simenon, for he is undoubtedly the master on the subject. I often forget the actual plot of his stories after I've read them – it's the mood that stays with me, that continues to resonate long after I have put the book down.

Interestingly, this quote is the opening passage from *Maigret and Society* and it appears to break one of Elmore Leonard's writing rules: never open a book with the weather.

Leonard is right: weather *on its own* is dull. What Simenon does here is create atmosphere by referring to the weather, or the season; he doesn't actually talk about the weather itself. What we get is a sense of happy nostalgia, of budding springtime and adolescence, and perhaps a hint of sexual awakening.

Many of these associations, of course, are being made inside the reader's head (in this case mine; you may be drawn to think of other things). This brings us to the main point about atmosphere: it cannot be implanted or imposed; has to be invoked. When it comes to the mood of a book, engagement with the reader's own imagination is essential. Which means enough information has to be put across to trigger it, but not so much that it gets swamped (or the pace of the novel suffers).

In the end, it's about using the right words – and only a writer's own judgement and intuition can say what those are.

The key here is creating resonance. You want readers to come away with a feeling – one which is alive as much in their own minds as it is on the actual page. To achieve this, lightness of touch is essential, but the details scattered through the text have to be the right ones – they have to have the power to engage with the imagination.

Often atmosphere is being evoked within the reader's own mind – subconsciously – almost from the very first sentence. If a book grabs us from the off, our imagination is set to work engaging with the new world being presented and *recreating* it in our minds before a single phrase dedicated to setting or atmosphere has even been reached.

> *Samuel Spade's jaw was long and bony, his chin a jutting v under the more flexible v of his mouth. His nostrils curved back to make another, smaller v. His yellow-grey eyes were horizontal. The v motif was picked up again by the thickish brows rising outward from twin creases above a hooked nose, and his pale brown hair grew down – from high flat temples – in a point on his forehead. He looked rather pleasantly like a blond satan.*

This opening passage from Dashiell Hammett's *The Maltese Falcon* is to all intents and purposes an example of characterisation. And indeed it is, but listen to what's going on inside your own imagination as you read it and you'll notice that an atmosphere is also being created: the details of Spade's face, the repetition of the unusual v motif, the use of words like 'bony' and 'satan'. Already we are in a hard, menacing world where the tiniest things – things that others might ignore – can have great importance. Watch out, we are being told. This is no everyday place we are entering and we need to be on our guard.

A series of reactions and connections has already been sparked within our own minds, so much so that at some level a picture of where we are is already forming, without a single line having been dedicated to setting.

Atmosphere is paramount, it has grabbed us from the first paragraph, and we are there, with Spade and his assistant in their office. By the time a passage of description comes along, over a page further on, it serves to confirm the imagery that has already been forming within us over the previous few lines:

The tappity-tap-tap and the thin bell and muffled whir of Effie Perrine's typewriting came through the closed door. Somewhere in a neighboring office a power driven machine vibrated dully. On Spade's desk a limp cigarette smouldered in a brass tray filled with the remnants of limp cigarettes. Ragged grey flakes of cigarette-ash dotted the yellow top of the desk and the green blotter and the papers that were there. A buff-curtained window, eight or ten inches open, let in from the court a current of air faintly scented with ammonia. The ashes on the desk twitched and crawled in the current.

Yes, we think as we read the passage. It's not as if we already knew this, but almost. The setting for the scene – Spade's slightly shoddy office – fits perfectly with the atmosphere already invoked from the first page. And it has all been done with great economy – not too much, not too little; just enough to draw us in.

The sounds ('tappity-tap-tap'), sights ('limp cigarettes', 'brass tray') and smells ('ammonia') have all been covered. To them, Hammett adds a fourth, no less important: a sense of impending danger and death, deftly elicited by the twitching, crawling ashes on the desk. He doesn't tell us straight, but we know: something horrible is about to happen.

I've mentioned these two books because they both illustrate an important point about atmosphere and setting: they have to be there from the beginning. In fact, the first few pages are where atmosphere especially has to be established. After that it will largely continue under its own momentum, aided by the occasional nudge, or perhaps nuanced or changed at various points as the needs of the story dictate.

And how do you go about establishing atmosphere? I don't think there's any easy step-by-step guide here: do this, that and the other, etc. The atmosphere has to be alive within the author; the mood is part of what the writer is experiencing as the words are written down. We're not talking about 'mood' in its shallower sense of 'feeling a bit annoyed', of course. Simenon's phrase about a 'poetic line' is probably cleaner and more helpful here. Once that's there, once it fills you and becomes one of the motors for writing itself, the atmosphere as passed on to the reader will probably take care of itself; it can't help but be expressed in some form.

But I come back to the point about 'lightness of touch': it's important not to overdo it. Not that you should worry about this too much during the process of actual writing: anything that's heavy-handed can be taken out during the editing process (top tip: write a whole first draft before re-reading or editing a single word of the text). Here, another of Elmore Leonard's rules is particularly useful: if it sounds like writing, rewrite it. If, when you're reading, you think, 'Oh, here's the bit establishing atmosphere', it almost certainly needs cutting out.

Atmosphere and setting are of course related, which is why we're discussing them together in this essay, but they're not the same. I've spoken mostly about the first; we should have a think about the second.

It's become a bit of a cliché in crime writing now to talk about the setting and location – let's take Edinburgh as a totally random example – as being 'a character' in its own right. There's a truth behind the cliché, however: the location where the action occurs will have a powerful effect on the novel, and subsequent series if it turns into that. The prevailing weather, type of architecture, the customs, language, mannerisms: all these are going to feed into the general tone – or atmosphere, again – of the book.

Of course you may move things around a bit, in which case you could think about how each setting fits with the section of the book in which it appears. Not just in terms of the mechanics of the plotting, but in terms of its mood. Istanbul, for example, has a certain melancholy about it; Venice can be suffocating; Lisbon feels like a point of departure, while New York is about arrival. How does the section you're writing work with the overriding sense of the place where events are happening?

Also – how much can you assume the reader knows about the particular location? Just writing 'Paris', for example, can be enough in itself to elicit a whole range of quite powerful associations. Is that good or bad, though? Do you want to set your novel in a place that most readers feel they know quite well? Some of those associations might make your job easier, but others might get in the way. It's worth giving some thought to.

My own crime novels are set mostly in Valencia – a city people have generally heard of but usually know little about as traditionally it hasn't featured on the Spanish cultural trail. That, for me, was a good thing: I felt as though I had a clean sheet on which to work. No assumptions or biases to take into account. The reader, I felt, would take whatever I said about the city as Gospel. (*Ha*! The sense of power!)

The 'down side', however, was that I felt I had a lot of explaining to do –

introducing the city, establishing a sense of place. I couldn't rely on people's previous ideas about Valencia. In the end, for the first novel at least, that was a complicated balance to achieve while keeping the story going.

And how is it done? Straight passages of description are fine (as the Hammett quote demonstrates), but should be kept to a minimum unless you deliberately intend to slow the pace down at specific moments in the story. Otherwise small details can be scattered lightly through the text to keep the sense of setting alive – perhaps the kinds of cigarettes people smoke, the food they eat (or the time of day that they eat it), or the quality of the light. Almost any local detail can work if used in the right way.

The orthodoxy says you should write about what you know, and when it comes to setting there's an obvious advantage there. But it's worth bearing in mind that you may know a place too well, that over-familiarity may render you incapable of portraying it effectively to those who have never been there. Can you get some perspective on your setting? Are you good at describing it to people who don't know it?

If not, you might want to change. Setting is hugely important if you're thinking about a series of novels. It has to be a place that you're happy going back to time and again. Are you going to get bored by it? Will you run out of things to say about it after the first novel?

Another thing to think about is this: today, with so much information at our finger-tips, it's not beyond the realms of possibility to write about a place you've never even travelled to. Why not? Give it a go. It might be a liberating experience.

It's only apt that in an essay about crime writing there should be some 'bullet' points. So here we are, summing up a little:

- In terms of atmosphere, keep it light: less is more
- The mood of the book should be instinctive and organic. If you're thinking about it too much something is probably going wrong
- Try to establish mood on the first page(s) – but again, don't worry too much about it while you're writing: everything and anything can be changed during the editing process
- Setting is important: how much do you know about the place? How much can you assume readers know? Is it only for one book, or a series? How does the overall atmosphere of the place work with the action you're setting there?
- Lack of first-hand knowledge of a city needn't be a reason for not writing about it.

Lastly, atmosphere is sometimes more than just a matter of an overall mood: it can hint at something more, be an approximation of a greater truth – often the essence of what you are trying to write. It may be clear in your mind when you start, or the writing itself may become the process by which it makes itself clear to you. Whatever your experience, listen out for it: it may turn out to be the engine for this and all your subsequent writing.

THE BULLFIGHT

THE BULLFIGHT

He'd broken his vow once. Now that he'd done it again he felt almost worse, but coming to this bullfight, he knew, was important: politically because it showed the *Policía Nacional* was still concerned about the appearance of finding Blanco's killer; for the investigation because the chances were significantly high that the murderer would be present, revisiting the scene, enjoying the spectacle of a bullfight in his victim's honour; and emotionally because Alicia had invited him. No, if he was honest with himself, whatever he felt towards her was only physical at this point; his emotions were in a state of paralysis.

The bullring was packed. Few tickets had made it on to the open market as grandees and aficionados from all over the country had hustled for a place at this, what had turned out to be one of the most important events of the year.

Cámara pushed through the crowds, his eyes darting from face to face, his senses alive and sharp. The sound of the beating drum from the Anti-Taurino League was barely audible above the din of thousands of people streaming through the gates and into the portico walkway that circled the outside of the bullring.

Alicia wasn't at the entrance waiting for him as she'd promised, and in the end he had to wave his Police ID at the ticket girl and force his way in – something he could have done anyway, but he preferred the idea of entering just like any other member of the public. Word would get out eventually that the policeman heading the Blanco case was there.

A hand grabbed his arm and jerked him to one side.

'You found it, then?'

Alicia was wearing a low-buttoned cream blouse with a high collar, and a tan suede jacket. Gold earrings with shiny red gemstones dangled at either side of her exposed neck. She smiled at Cámara.

'Our seats are just here. We need to go: it's about to start.'

She led Cámara by the arm down a wide tunnel before they came out into the sunshine of the bullring. Stepping up a small stone staircase, they passed a gate of painted wood and went through to the very first row of seats, just above the *callejón* passageway where the bullfighters moved around the ring before stepping out into the arena itself.

'We couldn't be any closer,' Cámara said.

'Not unless you want to jump in and have a go yourself.'

They squeezed in among the other spectators and sat on a wooden bench with a proper back and arm rests. Not only the best seats for viewing the spectacle, but the most comfortable as well: a few rows higher up this level of luxury came to an end and people had to make do with stone benches, softened only by plastic-covered cushions hired from one of the stalls near the entrance.

Many of the men were wearing jackets and ties, while some of the women had come in black, or sombre-coloured dresses, taking advantage of the below-average temperatures to take their fur coats for one final outing before being mothballed till the following winter. The ubiquitous cigar smoke, hanging thickly in the air above their heads, was mingled with sweet-scented perfumes and rich colognes.

Yet despite there being a seriousness about the afternoon, the atmosphere was anything but solemn. A woman sitting next to him carefully placed her *mantón de Manila* – a flowery, embroidered silk shawl – over the barrier in front of them, as was the custom, and then pulled out a black-and-white photograph of Blanco from her bosom and pinned it to the top. She smiled as she did so: she was here to commemorate the life of a great bullfighter, more to remember him than to mourn his loss.

Cámara took in the rest of the faces around him, sweeping across the bullring to the other sections, glancing up and down: in the cheaper seats, in *Sol*, he detected a similar ambience: more men wearing hats; the women carefully made up for the event.

And all the while he was thinking: was *he* here, their man? Somewhere, among the thousands, he might be close by at that very moment.

The last spectators were taking their seats as the trumpets sounded and the *Puerta de Cuadrillas* – the main doors to the bullring – were opened. The first to ride out were a couple of men dressed in black velvet 18th-century-style costumes, with white ruff collars and long, elegant feathers quivering in their caps. They rode to just below the President's box, saluted him and then circled around the arena.

At his side, Alicia leaned in, pressing her body against his.

'These horsemen,' she explained, 'are the *alguacilillos*.'

'I've never quite understood what this bit is about,' Cámara said.

'It's a throwback to the past when bullfights took place in public squares,' she said. 'The city authorities – the *alguaciles* – had to clear the public away before the event could start.'

Cámara pulled out his packet of *Ducados* and lit one.

'Are you going to turn this into a lesson in how to watch a bullfight?' he said. 'I have a strong suspicion that you're trying to convert me.'

Alicia grinned.

'There's always hope,' she said.

Once the alguacilillos had finished, the main procession of bullfighters into the ring commenced. In the lead, their right arms wrapped in brightly coloured capes, came the three matadors, then behind them the members of their cuadrillas – banderilleros and picadors – followed by the *monosabios*, the picadors' helpers, the *areneros*, whose job it was to rake the sand after each fight, and finally the *mozos* with the horses used for pulling the dead bulls out of the ring.

Each detail of this was explained to Cámara by Alicia, but he had become more interested by one of the matadors at the front of the procession. Alejandro Cano was standing to the left of the trio.

'He'll be the first one,' Alicia explained to him. 'He'll take the first bull, as the most experienced bullfighter here today.'

Cámara pulled on his cigarette.

'Are you surprised?' Alicia said.

'Blanco took his manager away from him – a man who is also dead, but I notice no one seems to be remembering *him* this afternoon.'

He glanced at the spectators behind them – all eyes were on the bull-fighters in the ring.

'All I've heard about the two men is that they were great rivals.'

'Blanco and Cano were opposites,' Alicia said. 'But that's probably what links them so strongly. Cano the socialite, womaniser, very much a public figure. And a showman in the ring. He's aware of the audience in a way that Blanco wasn't. With Blanco there was just him and the bull. I think that's what made him so special: you felt, when you were watching him, that you were somehow present at a private, almost secret act of communion between him and the animal. He fought for himself, set himself against his own high standards, and that's where the spark for him came from. And it was reflected in how he was outside the bullring – never showy, always preferring to keep to himself.

'But bullfighting in some ways is about opposites coming together,' Alicia continued. 'The man and the bull, the brute strength of the animal pitted against the intelligence of the human.'

She placed a hand on his arm.

'Things that are apparently opposite are not always working against each other,' she said. 'Besides, Cano was there at Blanco's last fight: he's part of the Blanco story. Without him here this afternoon Blanco's memory would be ill served.'

Their conversation was interrupted by the sight of Cano passing through the barriers into the *callejón* and making a bee-line towards them, brushing aside with nods and smiles the people who were trying to attract his attention.

Alicia leaned over as he stepped up to where they were sitting and they kissed each other on the cheek.

'Chief Inspector Max Cámara,' she said introducing the two men. 'Alejandro Cano.'

Cámara felt a warm, welcoming hand shaking his: no cold sweat, no apparent nerves in a man about to fight an enormous, violent beast to the death. Cano was dressed in a deep burgundy red *traje de luces*.

'I wanted to thank you for your generosity the other afternoon as president,' Cano said. 'The ear you presented me was only partially earned.'

Cámara paused before answering: was the man making fun of him, or was this genuine humility on his part?

'I'm a poor judge,' he said at last. 'I followed my advisers that afternoon as best I could.'

'If you've come to learn more then you couldn't be in better hands,' Cano said with a smile for Alicia. 'There are few people – men or women – with a greater knowledge of bullfighting than Alicia.'

He reached out and grasped Alicia's arm in what appeared to be a naturally affectionate gesture.

'I'm still not sure how much about our national fiesta the chief inspector wants to know,' Alicia said. 'I suspect he's here more as a policeman than a potential aficionado.'

'Yes,' Cano said, the smile dropping momentarily from his face. 'I understand. Bullfighting is cruel. But for a person of sufficient sensitivity it can also be something else. Given the right moment – the right bull, the right torero, the right day.'

His *mozo de espadas* stood behind him holding his pink and yellow capote for the first part of the fight. Cano turned and allowed the man to open it out and then hand it to him.

'If there's anything you need, Chief Inspector,' he said before stepping away. 'Anything at all. Blanco was very dear to me. Ruiz Pastor as well. I feel their loss as intensely as anyone here. More so, even. We need to catch the madman who did this.'

He shook hands with him again, and then strode off, glancing out at the ring as the horns blew once again: the first bull of the afternoon was about to appear.

The first two sections of the bullfight passed without incident. In the *Tercio de Varas* the bullfighters tested the bull with their capotes, executing elegant *verónicas* and *chicuelas*, getting a sense of its strengths and tendencies. The more *bravo* the bull, Alicia explained in Cámara's ear, the more it would stand near the centre of the ring, dominating, challenging the bullfighters to take it on. A more *manso* bull would tend to stay on the outside of the arena, or close to the gate from which it had entered – the *Puerta del Toril* – as though trying to escape. All this would have a bearing on how the matador would fight the bull at the end.

This initial section ended quickly, however, the bullfighters retreated and the picadors came out on their well-padded horses and the bull was urged to charge at them. This part had always seemed the most meaningless and cruel to Cámara, the heavy picador pushing his lance as deeply as he could into the bull's shoulders, while around him the audience whistled and shouted loudly in protest.

'I agree, it isn't always very attractive,' Alicia said. 'But it's for two reasons. First to get a sense of how strong the bull is: does he charge headlong at the horse, or does he have to be coaxed to do so? And secondly you have to take some of the bull's strength away, to make him lower his head. Otherwise it would be virtually impossible to fight him.'

The whistling from the crowd intensified as the picador went to thrust at the bull for a second time.

'But the crowd don't want the bull to be weakened too much,' Alicia went on. 'That's why they complain at this point.'

'You aficionados talk about this being about a man pitted against a mighty beast,' Cámara said. 'But it seems the odds are always stacked against the bull.'

But Alicia wasn't listening, standing up out of her seat along with most of the rest of the crowd as the picador went for a third, and highly unpopular, thrust. Everyone looked up at the President, waiting for him to give the signal for this tercio to end. Cámara remembered having to place the white handkerchief over the edge of the balcony himself at this stage, but he'd merely been taking orders from the two sitting next to him, understanding little of what was actually going on.

Finally the sign was made, the horns blew, and the picadors walked their horses out of the ring, leaving the bull on his own. Time for the next section, the *Tercio de Banderillas*. This was the one part of the event that for Cámara seemed to have some kind of artistry to it, even if it meant further torture of the bull. With brightly coloured darts in their hands, about a metre in length, the toreros seemed to carry out a kind of dance in front of the bull, finally planting the banderillas in its back as they dodged within inches of its horns. This, according to Alicia, was designed to bring a bit of life back into the animal, the banderillas acting as a colourful spectacle meant to spur the bull on after the punishment of the picadors, before the final section, when the matador would face him alone.

The banderilleros came and went, and the bull stood in the middle of the ring, with red, yellow and blue darts hanging from his neck almost like a Native American's headdress. Voices were lowered as the final moment approached, the *Tercio de Muerte*. Cámara watched as Cano was handed his red *muleta* cape and *estoque* – the same kind of sword with a slight curve at the end that had been used in the killings of both Blanco and Ruiz Pastor – and stepped out into the sand. He stood for a moment in front of the President's box, with his *montera* cap in hand, asking for permission to begin, and then once that had been given, he started walking towards the section of the ring where Cámara and Alicia were sitting.

'This is when he dedicates the bull to someone,' Alicia said. 'He can do it either to an individual, or to the entire crowd.'

Cano crossed the sand and stood at the edge of the burladero just in front of them, looking in their direction. Cámara glanced around him to see who Cano was about to dedicate the bull to, wondering if it might be for Alicia at his side. He smiled, but as Cano stood there expectantly, he felt Alicia nudge him in the ribs.

'Stand up,' she ordered. 'It's for you.'

He felt several thousand eyes turn towards him as he got to his feet.

'You honour us by being here, Chief Inspector,' Cano called out from the arena, stepping through the burladero and handing his montera to him. Cámara felt the hat's tight curly astrakhan fabric rubbing against his fingers as he reached down for it.

'It is my honour to be here,' he said, uttering the first thing that came into his head. Then Cano held his arms out towards him and the two men embraced.

'I loved Blanco as a brother,' Cano said in his ear as the audience around them broke into applause. 'And I will fight this bull in his name.'

Cámara's attention was fully on the fight for the first time now as Cano crossed the sand again and focussed on the bull. The burgundy of his *traje de luces* stood out against the bright yellow of the sand and seemed to echo the blood that was dripping off the bull's back and falling in dark patches at its feet. Cano arranged the muleta and his sword and took a few steps towards the animal's horns. He gave a cry and thrust the cape in the bull's direction. At first it didn't move, pausing before pawing the ground in anger. Again Cano flicked the red cape. This time it responded, lowering its head and suddenly charging at him. Deftly, Cano swept the muleta to one side and the bull passed within inches of his body. Turning on his heel, Cano flicked the muleta towards the bull on his other side, and again the animal charged, pushing forwards with his horns, passing even closer to the man this time as Cano gracefully passed the cape in front of him, slowing the bull down, never allowing the horns to actually touch the cloth. Again a turn, and again the bull thrust itself against the muleta.

The first shouts of *Olé* were being heard from the crowd by now and Cámara could feel how the concentration of the entire audience was fixed upon the dance that the man and the bull were performing in front of them. What was most extraordinary was that Cano had barely moved from his spot, keeping his feet planted firmly on the ground as the bull was made to pass him first on one side and then the other, circling around him as though the man had become a pillar in the sand, dominating the bull, making it move wherever and whenever he pleased, in total control.

And as he watched, for a second, for a moment that was lost almost as soon as it came, something extraordinary happened. It was as if the division between Cano and the bull had disappeared, as though for a fleeting instant they had become one single being out there on the sand, unified by their fight and struggle: one entity separated not by their mutual wish to kill each other but almost as if by a kind of tenderness, a passion. It was as if, for a brief time, matador and bull were brought together and joined through something that felt almost like love. But it was not any kind of love that Cámara had ever sensed or been aware of before, nothing he had ever known. And yet it was there, binding them and making them one.

It came in a flash, one exceptional moment, and then was gone. But the entire crowd had captured it as well, and a roar went up. Many were on their feet, clapping already, shouts of *Olé* echoing around the ring. At the other side of the arena the band started up on a *pasodoble*. People shouted and cried out:

the maestro had come and shown them his best; up above, Blanco would be smiling.

The bull had come to a standstill, its energy seemingly gone, and Cano stood as close as he could before its once powerful and feared horns, thrusting his chest out, before spinning around majestically and making a sweep with his estoque. The audience cheered: the beast had been beaten.

Cámara felt as if he were in a trance. Something had just happened, something he struggled to identify or explain, but which had gripped him for a moment and then gone. It was absurd: the bull and the man were intent on killing one another; how could anything that was happening down on the sand have anything to do with love? Yet he failed to find any other word accurately to describe what he had experienced.

He watched as Cano went through a few more passes, wondering if it would come back, if he would feel the same, but although the atmosphere inside the bullring was now alive in a very special sense, it failed to reappear quite as strongly. By the time Cano pulled out his sword to finish the bull off, Cámara had turned his head. Something magical had occurred, but he didn't need to see this.

Minutes later, with two trophy ears in his hands, Cano re-entered the callejón. He handed the ears to his mozo and then walked back to where Cámara and Alicia were sitting. Hands reached over the barrier from the audience in order to pat him on the back.

'I'm glad you got to see that,' Cano said as he paused in front of them. 'Those moments are all too rare.'

Alicia reached out and touched his arm.

'Blanco deserved nothing less.'

EL CABANYAL

EL CABANYAL

Valencia has come a long way in the past few years. From being a slightly forlorn and forgotten relative in the Spanish family, the city is now the hottest destination, with a rise in house prices to match.

And with so much new-found pride in their home-town, you would imagine that Valencians would never again commit the architectural crimes of the past, that the knee-jerk cementing of the coastline and construction of characterless apartment blocks was a thing of painful memory.

We were wrong.

If you come to Spain this year, and are in the Valencia area, visit the old fishermen's quarter in the Cabanyal. Go there, because this working-class jewel of Art Nouveau style – officially labelled a 'protected historical zone' – may not exist in its present form for very much longer. If the Town Hall gets its way, bulldozers are set to continue punching a large hole through the middle of it to extend a modern avenue from the city centre to the sea, and not even a restraining order from the highest court in the land seems enough to stop them.

Founded in the 13th century, El Cabanyal has become the common term for what are in fact three neighbourhoods stretching north from the port – El Canyamelar, El Cabanyal and Cap de França – and owes its name to the rows of thatched fishermen's cabins that used to line the beachfront. Also known as *barracas*, you can see the remains of some today, with their characteristic steep roofs – formerly thatched – shaped like an upside-down letter 'V'.

Sweeping fire in the late 1700s, then growing affluence of the inhabitants as the port was expanded, meant that most were replaced by elegant two- and three-storey town houses around the turn of the century. The Moors first brought a ceramic industry to the Valencia area over a thousand years ago, and drawing on an ancient local tradition of covering facades with brightly coloured tiles, residents finished off their new homes in the styles in fashion at the time.

Art Nouveau might be the dominant flavour, but wander around the streets and you'll find anything from Baroque to Eclecticism and even a few examples of something approaching Art Deco. Residents will tell you that their grandparents weren't overly concerned with the purity of the design, that they simply used what materials appealed to them. A Mediterranean sensibility to light and colour and a certain degree of keeping up with the Joneses means the area is unique, leading more than one visitor to describe it as 'an open-air museum'.

Concentrating on maritime shades of blue, green and white, the tiles are often spaced to create a zigzag pattern, or a checkerboard, and the effect is vibrant and harmonious. On closer inspection you may find the face of a sea god staring out at you from above a doorway, or a mosaic depiction of *pesca dels bous* – a kind of drag-net fishing that involved pulling laden boats back on to the beach using oxen, a scene local artist Sorolla depicted in some of his Impressionist paintings.

This is a *barrio* for taking a slow stroll through, criss-crossing from one street to another, and getting to know what is still a working community with a strong sense of its own identity. Although officially an integral part of the city for centuries now, Cabanyal people still talk of 'going to Valencia' if they travel to the centre.

Start near the port end and wander along the Carrer de la Reina. This is the main artery running north to south; all the streets are on a grid system, with the houses oriented east to west to benefit from the cooling *Levante* winds in summer coming in off the sea. As you meander along, you'll eventually cross the Avinguda Mediterrània leading from the sea to the indoor market. This is where El Cabanyal proper begins, and the area most affected by the Mayoress's plans. And also the site of some of the most enchanting houses.

Find the Carrer Barraca, and the streets parallel to it, and let your eyes wander. (A quick word of warning – owing to years of official neglect and degradation, drug dealers have moved into the area. You're almost certainly safe, but it's best to be aware.) On the Carrer Progrès look out for No. 262 with its turquoise-and-white tiled facade, amphora designs above the windows in mosaic, and griffin-head drains running off the terrace roof. Opposite, No. 279, finished in green and white, is more sedate, but no less spectacular. Meanwhile, around the corner on Carrer Luis Navarro, the narrow fronting of No. 309 has been covered in *Modernista* tiles with delicate vegetal motifs in green and ochre.

Many of these houses run through from one street to the next. Get chatting with the locals and you may be invited inside for a peek. Large pitch-pine doors open up into living rooms tiled with more intricate designs, elegantly carved window frames and arched ceilings. Alternatively you can stay in one of them: the B&B Cabanyal is on Carrer Josep Benlliure Recently renovated, it is run by a friendly young couple who are more than happy to tell you all you want to know about the local area and its traditions. And they can put you in touch with a group who provide guided walks through the streets.

Good places to eat in the Cabanyal, particularly for fish, are not hard to find. The *Casa Montaña* (Carrer Josep Benlliure 69) is a former *bodega* that has become one of the best known restaurants in the city, not least for its vast wine cellar (a thousand different makes, and counting…) While *El Cabanyal* (Carrer de la Reina 128), which is right in the Town Hall's firing line, is known to be frequented by the very people who now want to tear it down. Meanwhile the *Casa Guillermo* (Carrer Progrès 15) is home to the 'Anchovy King'.

But my favourite is the *Bodega La Pascuala* (formerly at Carrer Eugènia Viñes 177, but now at Carrer del Dr Lluch 299), just a street away from the beach. Noisy, bustling and a bit grimy, it's an authentic neighbourhood bar with rows of dusty brandy bottles lining the walls, and it offers cheap, working-man's size sandwiches with names like 'The Republican' or the 'Bribe-Giver', and delicious paella on Friday lunchtimes. Perfect for filling up after a dip in the sea.

Yes, Valencia has come a long way, but as you knock back a glass of *Magno*, it's hard not reflect that the place you're sitting in may soon be a pile of rubble. The future of the Cabanyal looks uncertain, but while it's still standing, visitors have a last chance to explore this unpolished gem on the Mediterranean before it is destroyed for ever.

This article first appeared in The Guardian *Travel section in 2010. Happily, since its publication, there has been a change of administration in Valencia, and the Town Hall plans to bulldoze a large swathe through the Cabanyal district have been shelved.*

SPANISH TRUE CRIME CASE NO. 3

THE VAMPIRE OF BARCELONA

THE VAMPIRE OF BARCELONA

Barcelona in 1912 was a tumultuous city. A steady influx of people from all over the country – drawn to one of the main centres of Spain's nascent industrial revolution – was leading to rapid growth and social unrest. Opportunities were available for some, but what most newcomers found was yet more poverty and misery. Three years before, tensions between rich and poor had exploded in the events of 'Tragic Week', when local families bidding farewell to sons drafted into the army rose up against a wealthier class who bought their children out of forced military service. The authorities reacted in heavy-handed fashion, with the result of over 150 deaths and five sentences of execution handed out to the ringleaders.

It was against this backdrop that the city's attention focussed on the story of a local prostitute accused of pimping and killing impoverished young children from across the city. Enriqueta Martí would soon become known as '*la Vampira del Raval*' after the immigrant district where she lived, or simply as '*la Mala Dona*' – 'the bad woman'.

Martí had been a prostitute since she was young. Later she married an artist, but the union eventually broke down after she repeatedly returned to her sex work. By day she would dress in rags and go out begging, while by night she would wear elegant and expensive clothes and mingle amongst Barcelona's decadent upper classes. In the same year as the 'Tragic Week', she was arrested for running a brothel where she offered children under the age of fourteen to wealthy paedophiles. These same powerful contacts, however, managed to have the case against her dropped, and she walked free.

In the years that followed Martí appears to have carried on as before, while also engaging in a new money-making scheme: selling ointments and potions meant to cure, among other things, tuberculosis, the great pandemic of the time. Little did her customers know, however, that the ingredients she used in their preparation were unsavoury indeed.

For some time, people around the city had been reporting that numbers of children were going missing, but the authorities hadn't taken the claims seriously and had so far failed to investigate. Then, one day in 1912, a neighbour of Martí happened to see two little girls playing in the window of her flat at 29 Carrer de Ponent de Barcelona (today Carrer Joaquín Costa). The neighbour knew full well that Martí had no children of her own. Her suspicions were raised and she alerted the local police.

This time they were listening, and a group of officers set off to follow up the lead. When they entered Martí's house – on the pretext of searching for an illegal chicken run – they found the girls, one of whom, Teresa Guitart, was known to have been kidnapped not long before. Martí was detained. Subsequent searches of the flat turned up blood-stained children's clothes and body parts preserved in formaldehyde. Extending their investigation, officers searched Martí's former homes across the city and discovered human remains hidden there as well. A notebook in which she kept the names of the clients for her pimping services was also said to be found, although its contents were never revealed.

The 'Vampire of the Raval' was imprisoned; the case against her seemed clear-cut. Yet she was never found guilty: just over a year after her detention, jail wardens found her dead. The authorities issued a statement saying that she had died of pneumonia. Others, however, claimed she had been murdered by fellow inmates.

Or had she?

Recent research by two historians has cast doubt on this official version of Martí's story. Was she in fact turned into a scapegoat for all the crimes against children happening at the time – crimes that may have been carried out by wealthier inhabitants of the city? The only confirmed offence she committed was the kidnapping of Teresita; all the other claims against her were never proven. And it appears that Martí suffered from severe mental illness. Not only that, the cause of death was apparently neither pneumonia nor murder by her inmates, but cancer of the womb, a condition which had prevented her from having any children of her own.

All of which raises the question: if it wasn't Martí who kidnapped those poor children around Barcelona, who was it?

Today, the mystery of the 'Vampire of the Raval' remains unsolved.

THE BEACH

A BODY ON THE BEACH - PART 1

The green-and-white *Guardia Civil* patrol boat looked out of place so close to the shoreline. Its sharp cut lines and metallic sheen spoke of thrust and speed in a place where people sought the softening embrace of sand, the gentle peal of waves and the caress of the sun. Sitting there motionless, an invasive presence, it was unclear what was causing the greater disturbance: its own arrival, or what it had come for.

A couple of officers accompanied him as he walked down an alleyway in-between the row of cafés and paella restaurants and headed towards the beach. Along the promenade a few heads turned towards the sea trying to make out what was going on, but the terraces were filled mostly with early evening drinkers, children eating ice-cream, and overheated waitresses carrying heavy, laden trays through a tide of discarded straws and paper serviettes. Above their heads, palm trees arched into the humid blue sky, while yellow-and-white flags from the lamp posts rippled as they caught an unlikely breeze.

Ignoring the main entrance to the beach a few yards away, he skipped over the low wall and on to the sand. The presence of uniformed policemen among the bystanders seemed to confirm that whatever was going on was serious, and needed to be witnessed. Yet already different types were discernible, like competing currents of water: those moving away, not wanting to see; others flowing in. Behind their mirror sunglasses, the officers darted their eyes over the array of exposed flesh as they grimly maintained their expressions of serious business-at-hand. He, too, was conscious of rounded forms, of browning skin and wet black hair streaking over naked shoulders. But there was only ever one body for him.

A second group of *Policías Nacionales* was standing on the shoreline. He felt sand seeping into his shoes as the officer in charge saluted and held out a hand to shake.

'Been there at least half an hour,' he said, nodding in the direction of the *Guardia Civil* boat.

On the deck, he could make out the captain standing with his legs wide apart, a green cap on his head and his eyes shaded by the black binoculars he was holding up with both hands. They were so close that the two groups of law officers could almost talk to one another without needing to shout, but he knew without having to be told that so far there had been no communication. A stand-off. Whoever was first to breach the silence would later get the paperwork load describing every step of protocol, every detail of what happened next.

And all the responsibility if things went wrong.

The police officer handed him a pair of binoculars, the same Interior Ministry standard issue that was being trained on him at that moment. He'd already seen the body as he'd walked over the wide expanse of the beach, already sensed in his guts who it was, but nonetheless he focussed the glasses on the floating, bloated form as it lay still in the tranquil Mediterranean waters, exactly halfway between the *Guardia Civil* boat, and the *Policía Nacional* officers lining the shore, with a thousand sunbathers at their backs.

Half an hour, and still no one had made a move. The *Guardia Civil* captain would be wondering what would happen now that this more senior policeman had shown up. He'd be weighing him up, concluding, quite correctly, that being out of uniform he was a *judicial*, an investigating cop. And from the way the others in his group deferred to him, he was almost certainly an inspector, perhaps even chief inspector, although on the young side. Still, superior enough to make a call on this, to break the impasse.

So whose was it? A body out at sea was *Guardia Civil* property. On land, here in the city, a stiff belonged to the *Nacionales*. And this one just couldn't decide which way it wanted to go. Caught between earth and water, floating in a legal grey area in the unmoving, shimmering blue. He glanced down at his feet: other detritus from the Mediterranean appeared to have less of a problem finding its way ashore. The usual collection of driftwood, scraps of plastic, seaweed and used contraceptives had found refuge on the pale brown sand, discarded rubbish and waste from the ships in the port just a few metres away.

He trained the binoculars again on the body. A light westerly *Poniente* breeze was blowing in from the plains and flattening the sea, which stretched out ahead like a sheet of glass. No waves, no currents to push the body in either one direction or the other.

For a moment he became aware of the crowds behind them. There were the usual groups for a weekend in early July: couples, families, hard-core sunbathers, elderly men with their lives in plastic carrier bags and nowhere else to go, teenagers still feeling their way around their changing bodies, students pretending to revise for the September retakes. He saw that a large number of them had yellow-and-white rucksacks, the same colours as the flags further back: free gifts from the Church preparing for the Pope's visit later in the week.

There was another sound, though, another group among all these: the sound of light giggling mixed in with the occasional cry. There were children on this beach, dozens of them. Some with their parents, others in a small group from the El Cabanyal district just behind them. For half an hour police officers had been standing here watching a dead body breaking the surface while kids were still splashing in the water only yards away.

He took one last look at the floater, then up at the *Guardia Civil* captain, a rage willing itself into life inside him. Strictly, this was his. He should have sent a dinghy out there and pulled the body back out to the boat. But something about the man's posture, something about his appearance made him relent. There was a look about him he had seen before, something he'd caught sight of in his colleagues, and in himself on occasion, something that, at times at least, seemed to be growing more frequent: the frozen, almost death-like expression that came when real decisions had to be made, and responsibility taken. This wasn't bloody-mindedness on the captain's part, it was inertia brought on by the bureaucratic labyrinth he could see himself getting caught in if he took just one step.

Handing the binoculars back to the officer at his side, he slipped off his shoes and pulled the belt from around his waist band, folding his jacket and laying it on the sand.

'I'm going in,' he said. 'Send two others to come with me.'

A foreign backpacking couple were sitting up and watching from nearby. He walked over to them and through sign language and a few words of English, made them understand he wanted some toothpaste. Reluctantly, a white tube was handed over; Cámara checked the writing on the side, then slapped a thick amount just under his nose to create a protruding blue Hitler moustache. After ordering the two officers volunteered for the job to do the same, he gave the tube back to the bemused tourists.

Bodies fished from water stank. Most people simply couldn't cope with the putrid, rotten stench. Those with strong stomachs only managed to do so by disguising it with the one thing that worked: menthol.

A BODY ON THE BEACH - PART 2

It was still too early for the cooling Levante wind to come in off the sea, and the air was gaining the blanket heaviness of high summer, a white, humid haze blanching the azure dome of the sky. The Valencia city coastline was flat and featureless, and while at other times of the year the mountains to the north and south were visible, framing the sea view, now they would remain rubbed out until the rains of late September, leaving just beach and wide expanse of motionless sea, and the brightly painted cranes of the docks.

Already there were hundreds, perhaps thousands lying out on the sands, but they were mostly packed close to the sea, leaving open, empty spaces nearer the esplanade. He cast an eye out to the mass of exposed, bronzing skin, watching for any spasm of desire to ignite within him. There were slim, dark Gypsy girls from El Cabanyal, in tightly packed groups with their brothers and male cousins like a wall protecting against their precocious eroticism. Groups of lighter-skinned twenty-year-olds, the boys with tight stomachs, the girls showing off their 100-euro bikinis bought in the spring from *El Corte Inglés*. Mothers, like Susana, with young children, using the free space of the beach to compensate for their cramped homes. Women in their fifties and sixties, often in groups of two or three, sitting on deck chairs under a sun umbrella, playing cards, their lunch waiting in ice boxes underneath fold-up tables while their husbands walked up and down the shoreline with white hats and blackened, beaten flesh like the 5,000-year-old bodies they found in glaciers and showed in television documentaries.

How many topless women could he see from where he stood? They were always a minority on mainstream city beaches like this; the real nudists had their own places to go, out of town. But he liked to use it as his own unscientific social barometer: the lower the nipple count, the more conservative the mood. Only a few more days and the Pope himself was coming, and newspaper kiosks were being ordered to hide their pornographic magazines in self-conscious displays of piety, while the Town Hall was closing down any public acts by gay rights activists or pro-abortion campaigners. For some the papal visit would be cause to cover up more than usual, but for others it would probably push them to strip off even more, invoking a particularly Spanish stubbornness. He counted: one, two, three topless women. No more. Clearly the powers of darkness were in the ascendency today.

And no. He sighed: nothing in him beyond an anthropological interest.

Wooden decking led from the entrances to the beach, creating pathways towards the sea and giving the bare-footed protection from the burning sand and the broken glass that often nestled beneath the surface. He strolled out a few paces, looking out to where Roures's body had floated the previous afternoon. There was no sign of him or his dead presence now: everything back to normal.

Stepping off the boards, his feet sank into the sand. It was dense up here, away from the shoreline, and footprints left behind were quite visible. He could see dozens of them scattering around him, trails and clues that formed no pattern, made no sense, crossed over one another and were lost, erased or smothered by a breeze bringing drier sand from further down the beach. Children playing football? A father playing catch with his little boy? A couple arguing? It was chaos. A chaos of smudged impressions and remains. How could one recreate and tell the stories of what had happened here based on such poor evidence?

Nothing. The truth was they had nothing on this case. No witnesses, no DNA evidence, not even a clear idea of how the murder had taken place. And unless the Logroño police lab results showed positive for Roures's blood, they were without a clear suspect or even a motive. Roures ran a paella restaurant, a restaurant held in high esteem. He had a good relationship with his clients, his suppliers and even the local fishermen, if the stories about his illegal fishing lines were true. Cámara was in the dark, and his usual method of waiting for something to show up or come along had only brought him Roures's corpse until now. He was blinkered somehow, but couldn't say by what.

SPANISH TRUE CRIME
CASE NO. 4

THE PYGMALION OF DEATH

THE PYGMALION OF DEATH

Aurora Rodríguez's idea was that her daughter would be the model of 'the woman of the future', an example whom others could follow as they emancipated themselves from a sexist, patriarchal society. She would fashion Hildegart into what she considered to be the perfect female: strong, independent, atheistic and highly intelligent, a considerable force among international reforming movements of the time. And she succeeded.

Hildegart was born in 1914 after Aurora had an affair with a Catalan priest, apparently with the sole purpose of getting pregnant by him. The father disappeared from Hildegart's life after the first four years, but by then the little girl was already on the way to becoming the superwoman that her mother intended her to be: she was reading by the age of two, and writing only a year later.

By 1933, at the age of eighteen, Hildegart spoke four languages, had become the youngest lawyer in Spain, and was studying for two other degrees, in Philosophy and Medicine. She had been an active member of the Socialist Party, becoming vice-president of its youth wing, but had left after becoming disillusioned with its Marxist stance, and had become more anarchist leaning in her political beliefs. At the same time she had become a passionate advocate for sexual education and emancipation, and had written numerous books and pamphlets on the subject (the first of which was published when she was still only eleven). She also wrote extensively about her political ideology. Figures such as H G Wells and Havelock Ellis knew her and admired her work.

Hildegart was becoming a publicly recognised figure, hailed by journalists as a prodigy. Her articles, in which she argued for the rights of women, appeared regularly in several national dailies. She appeared set on a course which would lead to her eventual rise as a powerful reforming figure in Spanish political life. Aurora's work in creating her daughter in the perfect feminist image appeared to be bearing fruit.

Yet on the eve of her greatest success, the mother was worried: this highly intelligent creature she had produced was starting to question things, to have ideas of her own. Instead of putting on the drab black clothes Aurora put out for her in the morning, Hildegart started wearing more colourful dresses. She talked about moving to England, where she thought she could live a freer life. And she began a relationship with a young man who shared her political beliefs.

Aurora became more and more anxious that her creation was about to desert her, to veer away from the very specific path she had envisioned for her. She started locking her daughter in the house. When Hildegart managed to escape, Aurora faked suicide attempts to blackmail her into coming back home. Commenting on the ever closer relationship Hildegart was developing with her boyfriend, Aurora told a friend: 'My daughter cannot marry: to do so would be to sacrifice the mission she was given on this Earth.'

Soon, her paranoia was spiralling out of control, and in this frenzied state, Aurora made her fateful decision: on 9 June 1933 she walked into Hildegart's bedroom, where her daughter was sound asleep. Pulling out a gun, she shot her three times in the head and once in the heart. Hildegart died instantly.

'When a sculptor finds the tiniest defect in his work, he destroys it,' Aurora later explained.

At the court case, held the following year, so many members of the public wanted to attend that they had to hold the hearings in the largest courthouse available. Aurora was found guilty and sentenced to spend twenty-six years in a psychiatric prison in Madrid, where she died of cancer in 1955. She never regretted her actions and insisted till the end that given the chance she would do exactly the same again.

A CITY OF FINE ART

A CITY OF FINE ART

Describe to us an ideal long weekend in Valencia for indulging in the visual arts.

I would take a gentle and unhurried walk through the old quarter of the city, visiting a handful of buildings and museums that I miss when I am away.

La Lonja is the old silk exchange across from the central market, its walls decorated with surreal and occasionally erotic gargoyles. It was finished in the late 1490s at the height of the city's Renaissance splendour (the Borgias once hailed from Valencia) and has – correctly, I think – been described as the greatest secular Gothic building in Europe. Inside, tall twisting columns like coiling rope produce an effect which is both delicate and powerful. Next door, the Consulat del Mar building, from a similar period, houses a stunning wooden ceiling painted in rich reds and greens. Originally these were a speciality of Moorish craftsmen.

A few streets further on, the Cathedral is home both to the Holy Grail (engraved in Arabic and verified by Pope John Paul II no less...) and some beautiful 15th-century Italian frescoes recently discovered above the altar. The celestial images have a lightness and freshness not always found in Spanish art from the same era.

To finish, I would cross the old river bed to the Museo de Bellas Artes to see Velázquez's complex and engaging self-portrait, and works by 20th-century Valencian painter Sorolla. His large-scale pieces can be a little stiff, but the intimate drawings and paintings of his wife and children have an exquisite and moving tenderness about them.

This article first appeared in Country Life *magazine in 2015*

SPANISH INTERVIEW I

AN INTERVIEW WITH THE NEWSPAPER VALENCIA CITY

July 2014

(Translated from the Spanish)

What did you find when you first came to Valencia? When was that?

In the 90s. I'd just met a local girl. I thought it was a great city, and the people very upbeat. The place was a bit rough around the edges then, but you could sense that boom years were just around the corner and that everything was going to change.

Did it come across as a crime-ridden city?

All cities are focal points for the best and worst aspects of humanity. Valencia didn't seem particularly dangerous, but the great injustices taking place here were plain to see.

How would you define Max Cámara?

He's my Spanish alter ego.

What is Max's relationship with Valencia?

Cámara is from Albacete, as a lot of members of the *Policía Nacional* in Valencia are. But he doesn't particularly like his home-town and prefers to be here on the banks of the River Turia. Valencia is his home, and I think he'll stay here, but every now and again he has to travel to other parts of Spain for work or personal matters.

Did creating the character of Max Cámara help you to see Valencia with new eyes? Or is your view of the city the same as his?

Cámara has stronger political convictions than me. Deep down he's an anarchist (the third novel in the series is called *The Anarchist Detective*), and this outlook influences how he sees the city and what's taking place here. In his mind, many of the people who govern the city – politicians above all – are little more than a band of crooks.

Which are Cámara's favourite streets in Valencia?

In the last two novels (I'm finishing the fifth now), Cámara is living in China-town (*el Barrio Chino*). He used to be based in Ruzafa, but the work on Line 2 of the city metro system forced him to find somewhere else to live: the vibrations from the digging made his block of flats collapse. He always enjoys wandering the streets of the Carmen area, which is full of surprises and interesting details – and you never know who you're going to bump into next.

In your opinion, which are the most mysterious or creepiest places in the city?

Some of the streets in the Cabanyal district are simply frightening – and we all know why. The old part of the city has a certain mystery about it for the very fact of being so old, of course. And then, in the Cathedral, you have St Vincent's withered arm on display, like some prop from a horror movie… But I think there is more mystery to be found in those uniform and anonymous new houses which line the main arteries leading out of the city, like the ones on the road to Ademuz. What horrors are taking place behind all those windows with their closed blinds?

What inspired you to write a novel about killer paellas? Is it a comment on the paellas sold to tourists in the centre of town?

They're not killer paellas. It's about a paella chef who's murdered because he has a dangerous secret.

What are you most proud of, writing about Valencia?

That people from Britain and the US have a chance to get to know the city through my novels. I hope it's a more authentic version of the city than the one that's usually sold abroad, and that it reflects something of the reality of what it's like to live here.

Lastly, how would Cámara define Valencia, in one word?

Complicated.

SPANISH TRUE CRIME CASE NO. 5

LAST WOMAN DOWN

LAST WOMAN DOWN

Pilar Prades was born in 1928 in the small mountain village of Bejís, in eastern Spain. At the age of twelve she joined half a million Spanish girls in being sent away from her home to find work in the nearest city, in her case Valencia. It was 1940 and the Spanish Civil War had only ended the year before. If the war years themselves had been difficult, they were followed by even harder times in what is known as *la posguerra* – the years of austerity and hunger that dominated much of the decade.

Introverted, uneducated and with a hard cold look in her eye which unnerved many, Pilar found work as a maid in Valencia households, but was frequently given her marching orders by employers who found her presence uncomfortable. In one year alone she served in three different homes.

Then in 1954 a couple who owned a pork butcher shop on Calle Sagunto took her in. Enrique and Adela would take care of the shop while Pilar carried out her domestic chores inside the house. But with time, as their trust of her grew, they would call the girl in to give them a hand when things got busy. Pilar seemed to take a shine to her new role.

Shortly after, Adela fell seriously ill and became bed-ridden, suffering from vomiting, muscular pains and weight loss. Suddenly Pilar had to spend most of her time in the shop with Enrique, only taking time out to look after her mistress and take her bowls of soup.

But Adela's condition only worsened. The doctor scratched his head, unable to explain her illness. Within days she was dead. The distraught Enrique wanted to close the shop while the funeral took place, but Pilar persuaded him to keep it open for the day, that she would look after everything while he was absent.

When he returned from burying his wife, the butcher saw Pilar at the counter wearing one of his wife's starched aprons, smiling and chatting to customers as though nothing had happened. Enraged, and without giving it a second thought, Enrique threw Pilar out on the spot.

A friend, Aurelia, found Pilar a new position at the home of an army doctor, where she worked as a cook. Pilar thanked her friend, but Aurelia was unaware that the very person she was helping harboured a secret grudge against her: some time before, at a dance hall, Aurelia had been taken out by a man whom Pilar had had her eye on. Unwittingly, the cook was placing herself in great danger.

Shortly after Pilar's arrival, Aurelia fell ill with diarrhoea, stomach pains and swollen limbs. Her employer, a doctor, became alarmed and had her taken to hospital. But then his own wife became unwell too, showing the same symptoms as the cook. Tests were made, and arsenic was found in both women.

The doctor made enquiries: he tracked down Pilar's former boss, Enrique and questioned him about Adela. The dead woman's body was disinterred and arsenic was found in her remains.

Pilar was arrested and interrogated for thirty-six hours, denied both sleep and food. Her room was searched and a bottle of ant powder containing arsenic was found. Yet she didn't confess. When the case came to trial, her defence lawyer warned her that pleading guilty would save her from execution, yet still she resisted. The judge ordered her to be garrotted.

It was 1959. No woman had been garrotted in Spain for at least ten years. Appeals were made for clemency, but none came.

On the appointed day, the state executioner, Antonio López Guerra, was called in to do his duty. But when he discovered that his victim was a woman, he flatly refused. Several hours passed, the prison authorities desperately waiting for a call from Madrid relieving them of their gruesome task. In her dark final hours, Pilar screamed out that she was still too young to die, that she wanted to live.

No call came. Someone produced a bottle of brandy and poured it down Antonio's throat. Drunk and now persuaded of his duty, he went in to see Pilar.

'Haven't you got a wife?' she cried to him. 'Haven't you got a daughter?'

Antonio did have a wife and daughter, and again he refused to do it.

But by now it was daytime. Pilar had been scheduled to be executed at six that morning, before sunrise. It was clear now there would be no clemency for her.

Moments later, she was dragged out from her cell to the execution chamber. Behind her, two guards dragged the drunk and distraught executioner himself to carry out his macabre task. Finally, with only one and a half turns of the screw, Pilar's neck was broken and her life ended.

But the story didn't end there: word got out about the awful conditions of her execution. One of the people to hear the story was Luis Berlanga, the film director. It inspired him to make one of his most celebrated works, *El Verdugo* – The Executioner. If you haven't seen it, look it up. And pay special attention to the final scene…

PHOTO ESSAY
THE VALENCIA OF MAX CÁMARA

"The key (or the clue) is closer than it seems"

DE TORRENT
ENTRADA GRATUITA
PARC CENTRAL
DE TORRENT
ENTRADA GRATUITA
ALQUILO TRASTERO
647 526 256
AGOSTO SEPTIEMBRE
TODO AL 50%
Club
PARIS
ABIERTO A PARTIR DE LAS 16:00 H.
CV-3007 km. 1,1 (antigua N-340)- Puzol - Sagunto
www.clubparis.es   Tel. 96 266 32 42
ENTRADA GRATUITA
ANTICIPADA 15€ WWW.DISCOTECAMASIA.COM
MASIA MASIA
LOCO FESTIVAL LOCO FESTIVAL

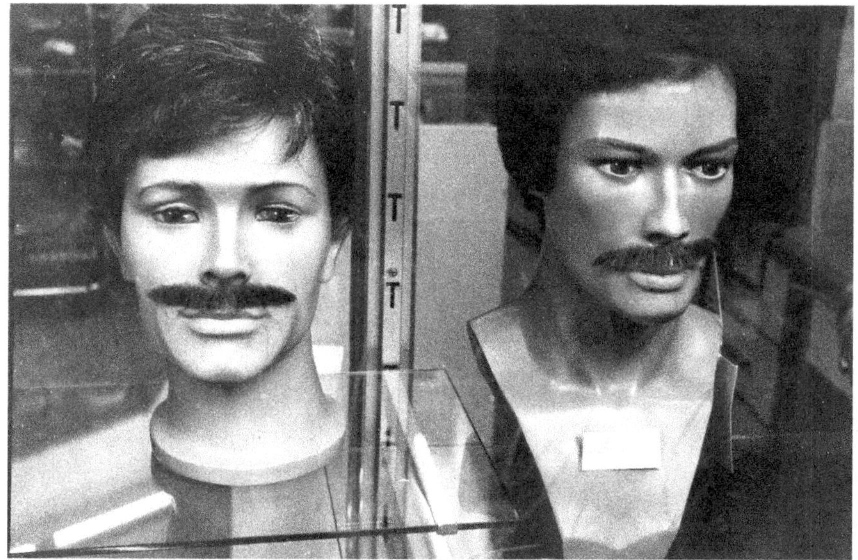

CARRER
DEL
PROGRÉS
CARRER

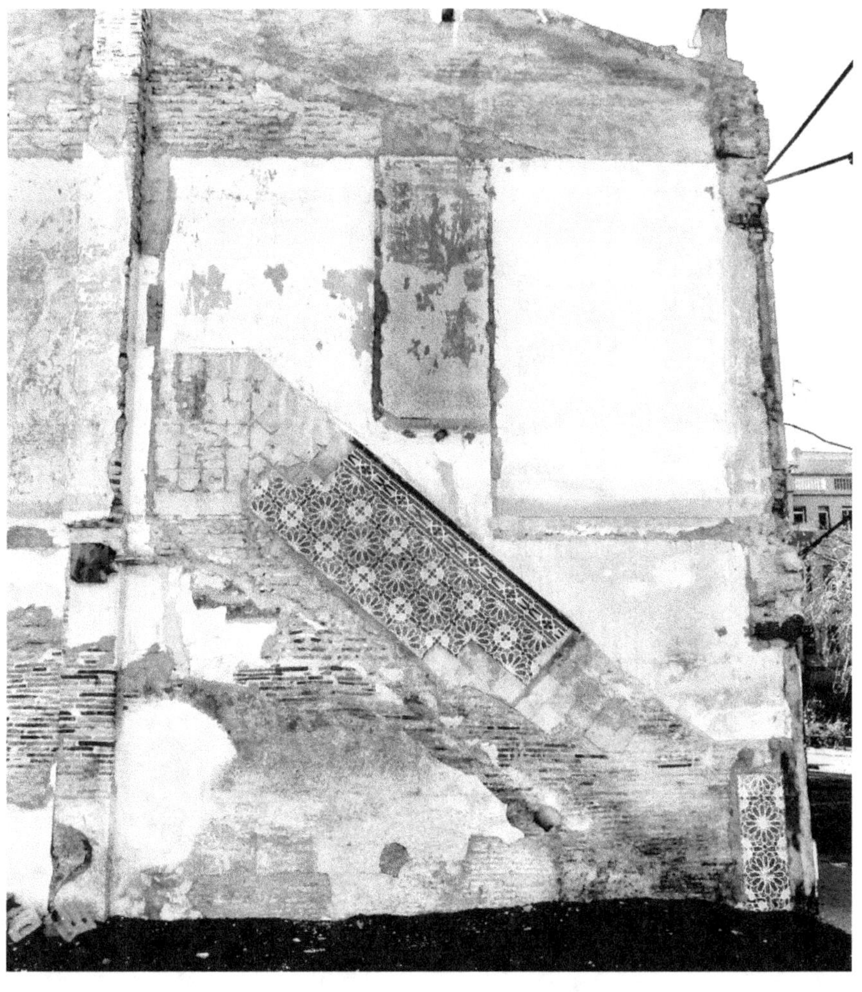

AVENIDA DEL
CAUDILLO

CREATE

FIGURA...
en 1 semana
¡en tu FARMACIA!

ZONA PEATONAL
EXCEPTO CARGA Y DESCARGA
DE 7 A 11 H. AUTORIZADOS Y
BICICLETAS CIRCULANDO
SO HUMANO

SPANISH TRUE CRIME CASE NO. 6

THE ASSASSINATION OF CARRERO BLANCO

THE ASSASSINATION OF CARRERO BLANCO

It's 20 December, 1973: the Franco dictatorship is in its final phase. Within two years the *Caudillo* will be dead and Spain will be entering a delicate period of transitioning to democracy. Yet in 1973 all this is a long way off and a far-from-certain eventuality. The ageing Franco has absented himself from the day-to-day running of the country, leaving the business of government in the hands of one of his most trusted men, Admiral Luis Carrero Blanco, prime minister, hardliner, and the person expected to continue at the helm of a repressive regime once the dictator himself passes away. But others have different ideas.

Since the 1960s, the armed Basque separatist group ETA, condemned as terrorists by the Spanish government, has been waging its own war against the authorities. Its targets have largely been policemen and members of the *Guardia Civil*, but now it's aiming higher.

In the evening of 19 December, two ETA members of the unit known as the *Comando Txikia* arrive at 104 Calle Claudio Coello in the Salamanca district of Madrid. They are disguised as electricians and start laying out some wires with the excuse that a sculptor in the basement flat needs more power for his workshop. In reality, the flat has been rented out by ETA themselves in preparation for what is about to take place. From the flat, they have spent five months digging a tunnel extending out beneath the street. This is now filled with 80 kg of Goma-2 explosives.

At eight o'clock the next morning, the wires laid out the evening before are connected to a battery. Meanwhile, a third ETA member double parks an

Austin 1300 outside No. 104, meaning that any cars trying to squeeze past will have to slow down.

Forty-five minutes later, Prime Minister Carrero Blanco leaves his home not far away and is driven in an official bullet-proof Dodge to hear mass – as is his morning routine – at the Church of San Francisco Borja, on Calle Serrano.

At nine o'clock, the two ETA members disguised as electricians take up positions on either side of Calle Claudio Coello, a few metres further up from No. 104. Just over half an hour later, Carrero Blanco's car turns into the street, with the prime minister having finished his religious observances and now heading to his offices. The driver sees the Austin double parked ahead of them and indicates that he is about to pull out in order to go past it.

At thirty-six minutes past nine, one of the 'electricians' signals to the other that Carrero Blanco's car has slowed and is now in line with the parked Austin. His companion reaches for a detonator hidden inside a briefcase and activates it.

There is a huge explosion, which is heard over most of the city. So much dust and smoke is produced that the members of the prime minister's escort car, which is behind, cannot see what has happened. Amid the chaos, voices are heard calling out that there has been a gas explosion. Only as the dust begins to settle does it become clear what has just occurred: Carrero Blanco's car has vanished, and in its place is a crater in the middle of the street ten metres across and seven metres deep.

Ten minutes later, the prime minister's car is finally located: despite weighing some two tonnes, it has been blown over 20 metres in the air by the force of the explosion and has landed on an inner balcony of the courtyard of a five-storey Jesuit monastery opposite. Inside, Carrero Blanco, his police bodyguard and driver are still alive, but all three will die of their wounds shortly after.

At first the government speculated about a gas explosion being the cause, but when ETA put out a communiqué claiming responsibility, they had to admit that the prime minister had been assassinated. It was a huge blow and an embarrassment for a government which had been built on armed force and being more violent than its opponents. ETA said its aim had merely been to remove one of the most reactionary members of the Francoist regime and an irreplaceable piece in its continuity once Franco himself was dead – an eventuality which was clearly on the horizon. Given this statement, and the complexity of such an assassination attempt, it did not take long for suggestions to be made that ETA had not acted alone. Years later the Soviet Union claimed the CIA had been involved. In 2008, declassified documents from the US Embassy in Madrid showed that in the months before the attack, Washington's representative in Spain had expressed alarm over how things might develop in the country once the inevitable happened, concluding that the best thing would be for Carrero Blanco to disappear from the scene. ETA flatly denied any CIA involvement, yet the Txikia group had received crucial details about Carrero Blanco's movements – which had allowed them to carry out the assassination – from a mysterious source. The only member of the group who had seen this person – and who might have identified them – was himself assassinated in 1979 by Spanish right-wingers, taking his secret with him.

PAELLA

THE REAL THING

Valencia has been a home, a base, a destination and a memory for me over the past twenty years. It is the setting for half a dozen of my books – the Max Cámara detective crime novels. I have learnt its language (Valenciano – don't ever suggest a Valencian speaks Catalan…), its customs, its mannerisms and its cuisine; I have leapt naked from its coffee-brown sandy beaches into the salty waters of the Mediterranean; suffered near-permanent ear damage from the explosive madness of its rite-of-spring *Mascletà* fire-cracker concertos; and learnt in the orange groves of the surrounding countryside how to make authentic *paella valenciana*.

For centuries, Valencia has been a black sheep within the complicated family that is Spain. Overshadowed by Barcelona to the north and Madrid to the west, it has been an underdog through much of the country's history: aristocratic Arab families of Al-Andalus sneered at their Berber coreligionists who tended to settle there; it chose the losing side in the 18th-century War of Spanish Succession; and Franco deliberately neglected it after his Civil-War victory in 1939, never forgetting that the city had been his enemies' capital for a lengthy period during the conflict. Ask an average Spaniard today what they think about the various regions that make up the country, and you will usually hear a begrudging respect expressed for, say, Andalusia, Galicia, the Basque Country and the rest. But when it comes to Valencia the attitude is more disdainful. Catalans look down their noses at their 'less-sophisticated' cousin to the south, while gravitas-obsessed Castilians find Valencian joie de vivre superficial.

And yet this overlooks the great achievements of the city. Some of the most influential sons of Spain have hailed from Valencia: before becoming (infamous) popes, the Borgias were archbishops there; some of the leading lights of the Spanish Renaissance, not least the 'father of modern psychology' Luis Vives, were Valencian; while it was a Valencian Jew, Luis Santángel, who stumped up the cash for Columbus's not-insignificant hop across the Atlantic back in 1492. In addition, it is Valencia which has given Spain what has now become its national dish – the afore-mentioned paella.

Paella is more than just a plate of food in Valencia: it is a ritual, a passion, a statement of identity and a dish of near-religious importance. At a wedding, you eat paella. When a baby is born, you eat paella. When a family gets together on a Sunday afternoon, they eat paella. No special event is complete without it, nor without the inevitable arguments about how it's made correctly and what the accepted ingredients are. Take it from me, as a reformed paella-extremist, Valencians take it very seriously.

And that is because in so many ways it symbolises and defines the city's culture and essence. On its land-ward side, Valencia is surrounded by the lush plains of *La Huerta*, one of the most fertile areas on Earth. So rich is the soil there that typically three crops a year can be harvested from its fields; traditionally just a small piece of land would be enough for a family to feed itself almost all year round. Meanwhile, just to the south of the city, the marshlands of *La Albufera* were where the Arabs first introduced large-scale rice-growing to Europe, over a thousand years ago. Combine these, and you get the basic ingredients of paella: beans from the horticultural belt and rice from the paddies constructed by the Moors. Throw in some chicken, rabbit and rosemary, and the paella is practically done. (Those scratching their heads at this point, asking where the seafood is, have been led astray by heretics into thinking paella is some kind of 'surf n turf' dish. Nothing could be further from the truth.)

Taking things one step further, you will find paella-purists who insist that the dish can only be cooked over an open fire using the wood from pines and local orange trees, while dried orange peel should be used as the initial fire-lighter. And of course, only Valencian water can be used in the preparation. I have known Valencians fill large water containers and drive them halfway across Europe just so they can make an 'authentic' paella once they reach their destination.

Yet paella's importance is more than just being a symbol of the fertile countryside on which the city's wealth was originally built: the dish is created out of essentially humble ingredients (with the exception of saffron, ever harder to find as it gets cut, like illicit drugs, with fake alternatives). But when put together and cooked in the right way, something extraordinary happens: they harmonise, as if in an alchemist's crucible, to create something far greater than the sum of its parts. On the one level, paella – like Valencia itself – is a seeming hodge-podge of disparate and even contradictory elements. But combined these can, at times, produce something magical.

Go there and try it for yourself. A recommendation? La Pepica, an old haunt of Hemingway's by the beach. Once you've tasted the real thing, you'll never be the same again.

This article first appeared in National Geographic *in 2020*

THE ANATOMY OF PAELLA

The restaurant had half a dozen tables outside on the pavement, where two couples of partially clothed northern Europeans were grilling themselves in the sun. Glancing at them with incomprehension, he ducked his head under the canopy and dived into the air-conditioned refuge inside.

He'd texted Torres earlier, and was pleased to see him already sitting there at their favourite table in the corner. It was a small place that did a decent lunch for seven euros – three courses with bread, wine and coffee. And best of all, you could smoke. Some kind of anti-smoking law had been passed a few years before, but it only applied to places with more than a hundred square metres of floor space. Anything smaller could opt out. So on paper the country could say it was conforming with the EU directive, while in practice everyone carried on as before. Or at least until they got caught and had to bring in a new law plugging the gap in the old one.

'They'll get us in the end,' Torres liked to say. 'You mark my words. We'll have to step outside between courses to spark up. As if we didn't have it bad enough at work. You won't be able to walk on the pavements for all the smokers blocking the way. Then people'll start getting run over, 'cause they're having to walk in the street where the cars are. And they call it progress.'

'Bad day?' Cámara asked.

'Ah, nothing,' he said with a sneer.

Cámara ordered a bottle of *Mahou* lager; Torres opted for some red wine, which came chilled in a half-litre flask, condensation thick on the outside of the glass.

'Bring me some lemonade as well,' he called to the waiter. 'Might as well mix it into a *tinto de verano* – a summer red wine. This stuff's undrinkable otherwise.'

They both ordered paella for the first course. Usually, as he grew accustomed to the intense heat of early summer, his appetite would wane for a few weeks, as though his body were slowing down to adapt. But today he felt hungry, perhaps, he reflected, because he had nowhere to go, no home to embrace him at the end of the day. So a feast-or-famine instinct had awakened in him, intent on gorging while food was available.

This being a working lunch, the paella came heaped on plates rather than served in the paella pan. Cámara looked down at the dark yellow mixture of rice, chicken, rabbit, green beans and red peppers and was pleased to see there were plenty of specks of brown *socarraet* in there as well – the crispy, gooey bits from the bottom of the paella dish where the rice was more toasted, and the flavours more concentrated. It was one of the things about paella they only really got right in Valencia, and they knew him well enough in the restaurant now for him not to have to ask for it.

And despite the fact that they weren't eating it straight from the pan, he still used the more traditional spoon to feed himself. Paella just wasn't paella with a fork.

The first mouthful was delicious: enough oil as a vehicle for the myriad tastes, but the rice was still a little chalky and not overdone. Paella, he often thought, was best regarded as a combination of pan-frying and boiling: both were needed to create this unique dish.

'There's a kind of rating system for rice dishes,' Torres said. 'All part of the mystery of paella.'

'You're not going to get mystical on me, are you?'

'Paella's not just food for a Valencian; it's a way of life.'

Torres took a swig of his fizzy red drink and pursed his lips.

'You know all this already. Or at least you should do. Been here long enough.'

'All right.' Cámara held up his hands. 'No disrespect. So what's this rating system, then?'

'*Bò, rebò* and *mèl.*' Torres flicked out his fingers as he listed the words. 'It's like giving marks to the paella depending on how good it is.'

Cámara chuckled.

'Serious stuff.' Torres stared at him. 'A family can spend the whole mealtime arguing over what grade to give it.'

'All right, so what do they mean.'

Torres gave him a look.

'*Bò*, as you should know by now, is Valencian for "good". *Rebò* means "very good".'

'And *mèl?*'

'*Mèl* means "honey".'

'That's the top mark?'

Torres frowned.

'Kind of.'

'Well is it or isn't it?'

'There's another one above that. But it's hardly ever used. Perhaps never. It belongs to the perfect, archetypal paella, like some kind of Platonic ideal. One that's been made over an open fire, using only wood from an orange tree.'

'And using Valencian water.'

'Of course. It's impossible to make paella with water from anywhere else. Doesn't come out the same.'

'And this top mark is?'

'*De categoría,*' Torres said, his Valencian accent thickening slightly, all open vowels like a yowling cat.

'You think Plato had paella in mind when he was coming up with his theory of Forms?'

'There's a Form for everything,' Torres hit back. 'Even the hairs in your nose, *hijoputa* – you son of a bitch. Or at least that's what my mate Joaquín told me at school. I never did listen much in philosophy classes.'

Cámara lifted up a spoonful of rice and meat.

'So what category's this one then? I reckon it's pretty *mèl*.'

'Get out of here. You don't know what you're talking about. This?' He pointed at his plate and frowned in concentration. '*Bò*. You can't give it more than that.'

Cámara put the spoonful in his mouth. It tasted all right to him. Perhaps a little heavy on the oil, now he thought about it.

'So what's below *bò*, then? What happens if it's a bad paella?'

Torres scowled.

'No such thing,' he said.

SPANISH TRUE CRIME
CASE NO. 7

MURDER OF A MARQUIS

MURDER OF A MARQUIS

Shortly before he was found dead in his prison cell in 1988, Rafael Escobedo, the only person convicted for the murder of the Marquises of Urquijo, told a television reporter that very soon he would reveal everything: the details of who and what was really behind a crime which had fascinated the entire country. 'The whole truth will soon become known,' he said. But just weeks later he was dead, and whatever secrets he had were never revealed.

The Marquises of Urquijo had been murdered eight years before, in August 1980, while lying in their beds at home in the exclusive Madrid district of Somosaguas. Both had been shot in the head with a .22 pistol. When police went to investigate, they noted that nothing had been stolen from the house: whatever the motive for the killings had been, it wasn't robbery.

The detectives widened their enquiries, and started looking into the family of the murdered couple. It didn't take them long to discover that the Urquijo family had been far from harmonious. The Marquis himself was notoriously mean, while his wife had always imposed strict Catholic discipline on their two children – Juan, now aged twenty-four and Miriam, twenty-two. Juan was living in London, having moved there after a violent argument with his father. Meanwhile, Miriam had recently separated from her husband – none other than Rafael Escobedo – and had started a relationship with an American, Richard Dennis. All these figures now became suspects in the investigation, along with the Marquis's estate manager, a man called Diego Martínez.

Within six months, in early 1981, police efforts were focussing almost entirely on Escobedo, having ruled out the involvement of the others.

Escobedo was know to have blamed his former parents-in-law for the break-down of his marriage to Miriam: this appeared to give him a possible – if not entirely plausible – motive. Eventually, officers moved in and detained him. Once in police custody, Escobedo confessed: he had, he said, only meant to kill the Marquis, but the sound of the gunshot woke his wife and so he had killed her as well.

It seemed as though everything was wrapped up. But there were problems with Escobedo's confession: he couldn't tell police the whereabouts of the gun used for the murder; he could offer them no credible motive for actually wanting to kill the Marquis; and nor could he account for his whereabouts immediately after the crime. Not long after, Escobedo retracted his confession, pointing the finger instead at Diego Martínez, who he claimed had been acting in cahoots with the Marquis's children.

Nonetheless, the prosecution went ahead and Escobedo was eventually found guilty of murder in 1983 and given a fifty-three-year prison sentence. Protesting his innocence, he went on hunger strike and even tried to commit suicide – twice.

Then, shortly after giving the television interview in which he claimed he would reveal all, he was found hanged in his prison cell. Suicide was suspected, but the autopsy revealed elements of cyanide in his lungs, leading to the possibility that he had been murdered.

For years after, the television interviewer used to admit that the conversation with Escobedo had made a huge impact on him. And he – along with the rest of the country – was forever left with the doubt: was the man guilty, or innocent?

OUT OF TOWN

OUT OF TOWN

The motorbike fired into life and he wheeled it off the pavement on to the road before feeding into the traffic, crossing the old river bed and heading north through the city. A wide, tree-lined avenue took him past modern, square buildings, with shiny square windows looking into expensive, box-shaped flats. The most expensive homes in the city were in this area, with views over the new but already crumbling complex of museums and theatres that had become the symbol of Valencia. The City of Arts and Sciences had cost hundreds of millions, with large amounts of the cash being siphoned off to line the pockets of politicians and officials. Some of these were now in jail or facing charges, but not enough to remove the stench of decay about the city, its reputation as Spain's capital of corruption. It would take generations, and many more successful prosecutions, to change that.

He spurred the bike on, twisting the accelerator to push past the cars, finding gaps down the middle, speeding through traffic lights just as they turned red. Once he got past the old fishermen's quarter – the Cabanyal – he turned and rode up through the university campus before connecting with the motorway and pushing out of the city.

The sea to his left was a gently ruffled carpet of deep indigo, with barely a wave breaking its surface. A row of elderly men lined the sea wall, sitting shirtless in fold-up chairs and sipping cans of beer pulled from ice-boxes as the floats on their fishing lines bobbed up and down in the quietly rolling surf.

He peered up at an almost cloudless sky. The heat was rising and the wind pulsing through his clothes brought welcome relief to his skin, yet the air was still relatively clear: the humid haze of high summer had yet to come and the mountains ahead in the distance were clearly visible, green and lush after the late spring rains. He looked forward to breathing the lighter, drier air up there. He could be up at Sunset in less than half an hour.

He turned off at El Puig and entered the sea of orange groves to the north of the city. Their blooms had all but gone by now, replaced by small shiny green balls of fruit. He caught sight of a lone farmer tending to some of his trees, a straw hat on his head and espadrilles on his feet – attire that hadn't changed for centuries.

Cámara sped on, working his way along windy country roads, a slope rising as he began to reach the foothills of the sierra. The orange groves gave way to fields of carob and olive trees. After passing the town of Náquera, with its fin-de-siècle summer villas and neatly tended gardens, he broke out into the mountains, greeted by pockets of tight cold air sitting in shaded folds of the rocks, and the prickly, embracing scent of pine as the trees around him warmed and glowed light green in the late morning sun.

The nightclub was close, a few kilometres further on and up a turning to the right. Most people knew how to find Sunset, if they'd never actually been. You could see the building from afar, even, some claimed, from the city itself on the clearest days. It was one of those swaggering country estates that some newly-enriched Valencian grandee had built for himself in the early 1900s. Cámara suspected that the man would be turning in his grave if he knew what went on today at his former home.

He had been to other nightclubs often enough. For years, in the 80s and 90s, Valencia had been famous for its Ruta de Bakalao, the string of discos around the city where gut-thumping electronic music played through the night and well into the morning. It had been rivalled only by the Ibiza scene, a badge of pride among the city's youth, who decorated their Seats and Vespas with brightly-coloured stickers from their favourite venues. Now the Ruta itself was no longer what it had been, and many had declared it dead. Yet a handful of the old places were still going, names like Barraca and Bananas that were legendary among a certain generation. Cámara himself had taken mescaline for the first time inside the Barraca toilets, as had almost half the city in the 80s. The drugs had been cheap and of good quality back then; people were experimenting and having fun. The ugliness came later.

A culture of some kind had attached itself to most of the venues. The Face was the trendiest and most expensive, with a snob value that cut against the grain of what having a night out was all about. Barraca had its top-class DJs; Bananas its strip acts and live sex shows. Yet Sunset had always been different. Set apart from the others, high in the sierra and looking down on the fertile city plain, it had an otherness about it. Some said that it had become a favourite among the gay community. Certainly everyone knew – or at least assumed – that its owner, José Luis, was gay. Yet Cámara knew of women going there – he had overheard a group of Alicia's friends saying they had been at least once, perhaps several times. Others who mentioned the place would also contradict the rumour that it was strictly a gay disco. Anyone went there, and people of all ages – a greater range than at many of the other haunts. Yet what went on at Sunset was the subject of dark rumour…

SPANISH INTERVIEW II

INTERVIEW WITH THE VALENCIAN NEWSPAPER LEVANTE

March 2018, following the publication of the Spanish edition of *A Death in Valencia*

(Translated from the Spanish)

How has Max Cámara evolved since the first novel?

I think he's angrier in this second book. He's taken a few blows in his personal life and now in the second novel he has to deal with the consequences of them. He's also more politically concerned, but he's starting to understand things a little better, and himself as well.

Where did you draw your inspiration from for Max?

From nowhere and no one. Max arrived one day while I was writing, and there he was. Each book reveals new sides of his character, and as a result the series of novels turns into a journey of discovery. There's some of me in him, it's true – to a degree he represents my Spanish self, but not entirely, and we're very different people in many respects.

You use real occurrences in Valencia in your books, such as the visit of the Pope, or the situation in the Cabanyal area. Why haven't you written about the Metro crash [of 2006, in which forty-three people died]?

Sometimes I ask myself the same question. I suppose it's because when I was writing *A Death in Valencia* it was 2009 and the accident still felt quite recent, the wounds were still quite raw. At the same time, I wanted to create a distance between 'my' Valencia and the city where I lived. To talk about the Metro crash would have placed the series squarely in the real Valencia, and that would have turned the novels into something else, namely a social and political commentary. They have that side to them, but it's not their only *raison d'être*.

Nor do you use real names, for example when referring to the Mayoress.

If I did, I suspect I would currently be doing this interview from behind bars.

Does the threat to freedom of expression also affect novelists?

Absolutely. And it's getting worse. There are censorship laws in place whose existence is hard to understand in a democracy. Recent prosecutions make that clear. Criminalising those who think differently, rather than treating them as legitimate opponents, is a basic tool used by tyrannies everywhere, and it can be seen in operation today against such figures as comedians, rappers and politicians. Novelists write fiction, but we're not protected as a result. Censorship works best when it creates an environment of fear, and that's what's growing now.

Is a writer more afraid now than in the past?

Yes. But the threat doesn't only come from one direction. In the English-speaking world, the censoring tendency often comes from those who think of themselves as liberals or on the Left, but the desire to silence you if you don't think like them is equally dangerous. There are many – too many – in the literary world who only want to publish opinions which conform with their political point of view, and actively try to stop books from coming out which have a different perspective – even if those books are best sellers. I know of cases like this, and it has happend to me personally. Publishers should be the first line of defence for freedom of expression, yet many of them are turning into agents of censorship.

Is there a greater crime than murder?

That's one of those questions that I'm not sure has a clear answer. Would murdering Hilter have been a crime? Murder is clearly very, very serious. Perhaps the question should be whether we are capable of seeing the other serious crimes happening around us. Creating generations of idiots through an overdose of bread and circuses might be an example. Or allowing the rise of a new authoritarianism, which we can see all over the world.

Do events in the real world inspire you?

Always. What happens is that these then get filtered through my imagination, where whatever resonates or creates an echo is turned into something new. I also try to peer as much as possible into the future. In 2015, the fifth novel in the Max Cámara series, *A Body in Barcelona,* was published. It talks about a situation in Catalonia where separatists are about to declare independence, and of a violent response by the government in Madrid involving elements of the secret service. When the Catalan crisis blew up last year [2017], the situation was so similar that there were times when I felt I had stepped into my own novel, published two years before.

SPANISH TRUE CRIME CASE NO. 8

THE GIRLS FROM ALCÁCER

THE GIRLS FROM ALCÁCER

It was the crime which saw the arrival of a new form of television reporting: crude, highly emotive and aimed purely at driving up audience figures by appealing to our more lurid fascinations – what would become known simply as *telebasura*: trash TV. And the night it first appeared was 28 January 1993. The place: Alcácer, a small town south of Valencia.

That was the day after the bodies of three local girls – Toñi, fifteen, and Miriam and Desirée, both fourteen – were discovered near an abandoned house only a few kilometres away. For two and a half months following their disappearance, their families, and the whole of Spain, had been asking the whereabouts of the three *niñas de Alcácer*. Now they had their answer and, live on national television, journalists Nieves Herrero and Olga Viza, performing a special outside broadcast from the scene, prompted the distraught mothers and fathers to share their grief openly to camera with the rest of the country.

The parents' journey into Hell had begun back in November the previous year. The three girls, all friends, had wanted to go to a party at a disco in the next town, Picasent. They had been before, and usually Miriam's father drove them. But this time he couldn't, having come down with the flu.

So the girls decided to make their own way there: they walked to the main road out of town and started hitch-hiking. A few moments later, a car stopped and picked them up, taking them as far as the edge of Picasent, where they were dropped off and started to walk the rest of the way. Only they never made it. Just a bit further on, a second car stopped, and the girls got inside.

They had no reason to suspect that the driver and passenger, Antonio Anglès and Miguel Ricart, would do them any harm, but when they neared the disco, the car simply carried on without stopping. The girls started to scream. Anglès pulled out a 9mm Star pistol and hit them with it. Then he tied them up.

A few minutes later, the car pulled up outside an abandoned building in a rural area known as La Romana. Ricart and Anglès dragged the girls inside. There they raped two of them. Then, after a pause in which they headed off for food and drink, they returned and raped the third.

The following morning, after all five had slept in the house, Anglès pulled the girls outside and forced them to stand beside a pit, where he shot them one by one. Then the two men buried the bodies and went home, as if nothing had happened.

When the girls didn't return home, the alarm was raised. For weeks searches were carried out, but no trace of them was found. Appeals were made around the country. Everyone wanted to know what had happened to the Alcácer girls.

Then in late January heavy rains came. Beekeepers working near La Romana discovered bones protruding from the recently softened earth. They alerted the authorities. The television cameras arrived. The whole country waited with baited breath.

Near the scene of the crime the police found one of Ricart's gloves and an official document belonging to Anglès's brother. It was enough to identify the killers.

Anglès got away before he could be arrested, but Ricart was not so lucky. Picked up by the police, he was eventually found guilty of murder, rape and kidnapping, and given a 170-year sentence. He served twenty years of it and was released in 2013. His current whereabouts are not known.

It was later discovered that his accomplice, Anglès, had managed to hide before making his way to Portugal, where he boarded a ship heading to Ireland as a stowaway. Discovered by the crew as they were nearing their destination, he threw himself into the sea: the life jacket he was wearing was eventually recovered, but no trace of Anglès was found. To this day he is on Interpol's 'Most Wanted' list.

Anglès's disappearance combined with the enormously high media interest in the story helped fuel conspiracy theories about the case, however. Discrepancies and contradictions in the police accounts of events allowed many, including some of the girls' family members, to subscribe to a version which insisted that the three had in fact been abducted by Ricart and Anglès on the orders of rich and powerful figures who wanted them to appear in a 'snuff movie'. The supposed perpetrators were even named at one point by investigative journalists. They sued for defamation and won their case.

But the conspiracy idea, despite never being proven, remains. To this day, the father of Desirée believes his daughter's abductors were acting on behalf of others.

THE REAL MAX CÁMARA

THE REAL MAX CÁMARA

Sebas was an inspector in the Spanish National Police, and also a writer. A mutual acquaintance had put us in touch, given the overlap in interests between us: I had written perhaps two or three of the Max Cámara novels by then.

We quickly became friends, discussing books, police work, and the history of Moorish Spain, the backdrop to his novels. He was part of a group of writers who used to meet regularly at a bookshop near the Mestalla football ground; they invited me to come, and I gave a seminar on How I Write (a magic carpet, which I took along with me, was part of the presentation, I seem to remember).

And then one day, without warning, Sebas said simply: 'Would you like to meet the real Max Cámara?' He was referring to his colleague, the head of the Valencia Murder Squad. And of course I jumped at the chance.

We arranged a date and time – at the bookshop, which also had a café. He sat me down at a table – later I realised with my back to the door – while he took a seat opposite, and we chatted about this and that. Then, all of a sudden, he stood up, glancing in the direction of the entrance.

'Ah! There we are,' he said with a smile, indicating the person just walking in. 'The real Max Cámara.'

And so it was that I met Esther.

Over the weeks and months that followed, Esther and I would meet several times. She enjoyed the paellas my wife and I made on long Sunday afternoons that rolled, in inevitably Spanish style, on to late evening suppers: our *sobremesa* chats roamed over all manner of subjects, but the novelist in me always kept an ear open for details I might be able to use in future stories. Esther was a good raconteur, once she felt comfortable with you.

That day when we met, however, there was an initial tension. I saw a woman in her forties, of middling height, with pulled back dark blond hair, wearing gold loop earrings, large heavy bracelets on her arms, and light makeup. She had a look about her which stated in no uncertain terms that, should she so desire, she could calmly kick the shit out of anyone. We kissed each other on the cheeks and I sensed a hardness about her, like an armoured shell.

'So,' she said, boring into me with speckled, light brown and intensely penetrating eyes, 'I hear you're writing books about me.'

It hadn't occurred to me that in a male-dominated society, and in a male-dominated institution within that society, the head of a such an important department could be a woman. Which, of course, Sebas knew perfectly well. I laughed at my mistake, slightly uncertain, however, as Esther immediately came across as someone who didn't suffer fools gladly.

'I suppose I am,' I said. 'In a way. But I'd love to hear about what it's really like. From you.'

And she gave me a look: *her* look. When I think about Esther, it's always her eyes that come to mind first. There was so much going on behind them, a complex mixture of everything she was and everything she had been through. Seldom have I come across someone whose eyes were such a mirror of their inner selves, even while she tried to hide so much. It was as if, buried within them, were echoes of all the horrors she had seen and experienced – mainly in her career in the Police, but also, I sometimes wondered, from her own life. There were scars there which an outer layer of rock, steadily built up over the years, tried to protect – not least by suggesting that any hint of trouble on the part of others would be mercilessly crushed. You didn't get to become head of the Murder Squad without being both good at your job and as tough as they come. But at the root there was a tender and very human quality about her – perhaps the very thing that kept her doing her job – which could not help but be damaged by the day-to-day strains of her profession.

Sebas quickly smoothed things over: they were both work colleagues and good friends. I was a novelist, just like him. Slowly, as the conversation progressed, I could sense the sword and shield being lowered.

'Give me a call,' she said as we later said our goodbyes. 'I can show you around.'

And so, some weeks later, I got to see the inside of the *Jefatura*, the regional headquarters of the National Police, in the city centre.

In truth it felt like any state-run office block, with endless grubby corridors, scuffed walls, an occasional personal touch on a desk to cut through the institutional monotony. Except that there were more uniforms. And more guns. Yes, the guns… I was never brought up around them; I found them strange, almost alien objects. Did I want to pick one up? Yes, I did: it was a great detail I could use – a standard-issue Police pistol. But my hand trembled as I held it. Quite frankly, it scared me. After I'd noted everything I wanted to know, I put it back down, happy to break all physical contact with the thing.

She showed me the car park – where the top brass had the best spaces reserved for their luxury-brand SUVs. It was full; everyone else, including her, had to make do as best they could. The nearby streets were crammed with motorbikes parked on the pavements.

'A lot of police ride them,' she said. 'It's the best way to get around in a city overloaded with traffic.'

And then there were the cells.

'Down there,' she said, pointing to a dark, miserable staircase leading to the basement area. 'Do you want to see?'

This time, I admit, I shook my head. Something about the feeling of that stairwell was enough: accumulated fear, anger and violent frustration seemed to leak from the walls. I didn't need to see it: my mind's eye had already captured enough.

We went to a café across the road: nicely decorated, with a better quality coffee on sale: her regular. There were others nearby, but it was clear she didn't use them: rougher-edged places where her uniformed colleagues stood in groups at the bar, talking loudly over the noise of a TV set in the corner blaring out the days sports and news.

She pointed back to the Jefatura building we had just left, visible through the palm trees which divided us from the other side of the boulevard. Esther pulled out a cigarette and lit it.

'See there, the top floor, where all the blinds are drawn? That's where the head of Police lives.'

I couldn't help but contrast it with the basement floor reserved for the recently detained. Like a mediaeval castle, with the villains in the dungeons and the king in his lofty apartments. Nothing, it seemed, ever changed. Did she aspire to move up in the hierarchy?

She blew out a trail of smoke and grimaced. 'The money would be better. But it's no longer police work once you get beyond a certain point. It's politics.'

Policing was what she did, what she was good at. Why change to something else?

'My squad has a hundred-per-cent clear up rate,' she said. 'That's the best in the whole of Spain.'

It wasn't a boast, just a statement of fact. And I had no reason to doubt her: she was formidable. Woe betide anyone stupid enough to commit murder on her patch.

And did being a woman make a difference?

'It's an advantage,' she said. The waiter brought our coffees: black for me; cappuccino for her. 'Let me tell you a story.'

And so I got to hear about the Body in the Suitcase.

Some months before, there had been a murder: the body of an Ecuadorian man had been found on waste ground on the northern fringes of the city. When Esther and her team showed up, they were shown a suitcase. Inside, perfectly squeezed in, was the corpse.

In the real world – not the world of detective novels – the vast majority of murders in Spain are either crimes of passion, or to do with drugs and gangs. This one seemed no different, and the Murder Squad members all agreed. The perpetrator was clearly another male, and they should focus their search on finding him.

But there was something about it that made Esther doubt this. 'No,' she told her team. 'There's a woman involved. We're looking for a woman as well.'

The detectives took note. Within days the case was solved.

'In the end,' Esther told me, 'it was a couple. They confessed. The man was her husband and she was having an affair. Between them, the woman and her lover killed the husband and dumped the body.'

But how did Esther know from the start that a woman had played a part in it?

'Easy,' she said. 'The clue was in the suitcase. Getting a body to fit inside is no easy thing. Only a woman could have packed it in there so neatly in the first place.'

Then she gave me that look again.

'You see,' she said. 'It took another woman – not a man – to know that.'

THE END

THE END

He parked the motorbike, locked his helmet in the top box, then turned the corner of the street and headed down towards his flat. The prostitutes were out, looking sleepy and bored as they stood in the shade of doorways or smoked in groups of two or three by the side of the pavement. Cámara glanced up at the balcony window of his flat a few metres further on. The shutters were almost pulled down, but he thought he could see Alicia there, waiting for him. He had emailed before leaving the *Jefatura*, said he was on his way.

The sun flashed, reflecting off a shop window. He was blinded for a second and stopped, rubbing his knuckles into his eyes. When he opened them, he blinked, trying to see. Someone was standing in front of him: a woman. Was she trying to get past?

He stood to the side, but she moved with him. Then he took a step the other way. Who was she? There was something familiar about her, yet still his vision was blurred by the startling sunlight.

He raised a hand, blocking out the light. He saw blonde hair, a heavily painted face: clearly defined cupid's bow and pencilled eyebrows arching like black rainbows high into her brow.

Cámara stopped, his heart suddenly frozen.

How many times had he imagined this moment, only to dismiss it. The only policeman to live in the centre of the city. They all shook their heads at him: no other was prepared to take the risk of being easily found, of reprisals being taken against themselves or their families. The outlying towns and satellite villages were much safer. Only a lunatic like Cámara would be so stupid as to have a flat not only in the centre, but in one of the roughest areas. Yet Cámara hadn't minded. This was life, he thought. Anything else was unreal.

But he had never, in his heart, imagined this moment ever really coming to pass. There was, in his imagination, not fully recognised, a sense that he was protected in some way, that no serious harm would come to him. He had been wounded in the course of his policing years, it was true, but death had never formed a part of his musings on his position, his risk, his openness.

And yet, now, here She was: Death staring down at him through the coal-black eyes of Ileana.

'For Bogdan,' she said. 'For everything.'

He watched in silent resignation as she lifted the gun, pulled the trigger, and felt the kick of the explosion within the barrel.

And the bullet, spinning towards him.

And very slowly he put his hand out and lowered himself to the ground, just as Jimmy had described. In a world beyond time.

The sun itself reached out golden hands to catch him.

'Hello.'

He heard a voice. It sounded like Hilario, his grandfather.

'Wasn't expecting you so soon.'

MAX CÁMARA'S
FAVOURITE PROVERBS

MAX CÁMARA'S FAVOURITE PROVERBS

Dentro de la concha está la perla, aunque no puedas verla
The pearl is inside the shell, whether you can see it or not

≈

Para aprender, perder
Understanding comes with loss

≈

Hombre que el bien no agradece, solo el desprecio merece
A man who doesn't appreciate goodness deserves only scorn

≈

A veces los muertos hablan
The dead sometimes speak

≈

Lo que no mata, engorda
That which doesn't kill you makes you fat

≈

Por la boca muere el pez
   A fish dies through its mouth (Watch what you say)

≈

A veces caza quien no amenaza
   Sometimes the dangerous one is not the one making threats

≈

Bien sabe el sabio que no sabe. Solo el necio piensa que sabe
   A wise man knows well that he knows nothing. Only a fool thinks he knows

≈

Más vale estar solo que mal acompañado
   Better to be alone than in bad company

≈

Quien al mear no hace espuma, no tiene fuerza en la pluma
   He whose piss doesn't foam up has no lead in his pencil

≈

Quien duerme no vive
   He who sleeps doesn't live

≈

Quien peces quiere, mojarse tiene
   He who wants to catch fish has to get wet

≈

Donde comen tres, comen cuatro
   Where there's food for three, there's food for four

A cada cerdo le llega su San Martín
Every pig has his St Martin's Day (the traditional feast for slaughtering swine)

Aceite de oliva, todo mal quita
Olive oil cures all ills

A la cama no irás sin saber una cosa más
Don't go to bed without having learnt something new

Burro grande, ande o no ande
Just give me the big donkey; it doesn't matter if it can walk or not

A veces, lo que ocurre en un año ocurre en un acto
Sometimes the events of a year take place in an instant

Cree el ladrón que todos son de su condición
A thief believes everyone is the same as him

De viejo morirás y aprendiz quedarás
You'll die of old age but still be no more than an apprentice

Dime con quién andas y te diré quién eres
Tell me who you spend time with and I'll tell you who you are

＜

Dios aprieta, pero no ahoga
God pushes you down, but doesn't drown you

＜

El hombre es el único animal que tropieza dos veces en la misma piedra
Man is the only animal who trips up twice on the same stone

＜

El que resiste, gana
He who digs in, wins

＜

El tiempo es oro, y la vida un tesoro
Time is golden, and life is a gift

＜

La muerta, ni buscarla ni temerla
Neither look for, nor fear, death

＜

No sientes el tiempo perdido, sino el que puedas perder
Don't be sorry about the time you've wasted; be sorry for the time that you may yet waste

＜

Dar y perder parecido viene a ser
In the end, giving and losing are pretty much the same thing

＜

Más vale perder un minuto en la vida, que la vida en un minuto
Better to lose a minute of life than to lose your life in a minute

~

Quien bien come y bien bebe, bien hace lo que debe
He who eats and drinks well does his duty well

~

Por las obras, no por el vestido, el hipócrita es conocido
A hypocrite is recognised by what he does, not by how he appears

~

Oro es lo que oro vale
What's worth the same as gold, is gold

~

Una flor no hace jardín
One flower does not a garden make

~

Si tienes pan y lentejas ¿por qué te quejas?
If you've got bread and lentils to eat, what are you complaining about?

~

Quien habla, siembra; quien oye, recoge
He who speaks, sows; he who listens, harvests

~

Quien espera, desespera
He who waits, despairs

~

Quien busca, halla
He who seeks, finds

～

Quien anda con cojo, aprende a cojear
He who walks with a lame man will end up becoming lame himself

～

No hay peor sordo que él que no quiere oír
No one is deafer than he who doesn't want to hear

～

Melones y amigos, muchos salen pepinos
As with melons, so with friends: many turn out to be no more than cucumbers

～

Mucho ruido y pocas nueces
A lot of noise, but few walnuts (Much ado about nothing)

～

No hay mal que por bien no venga
Something good always comes out of a reverse (Every cloud has a silver lining)

～

Más vale ser cabeza de ratón que cola de león
Better to be the head of a mouse than the tail of a lion

～

Más sabe el diablo por viejo que por diablo
The Devil knows more because he's old than because he's the Devil

～

Los amigos se conocen en la necesidad

You find your real friends in times of need

Más apaga buena palabra que caldera de agua
The right word puts a fire out faster than a bucket of water

Lo que no se empieza, nunca se acaba
Something which is never started never ends

AN INTERVIEW WITH MAX CÁMARA

AN INTERVIEW WITH MAX CÁMARA

'So you made it.'

'This feels… familiar. As though I've been here before.'

'Right, I think we can begin.'

'And yet… I'm not sure.'

'This is important. We need you to concentrate.'

'There was a tightness, a constriction. Struggle. I was fighting.'

'That's not uncommon.'

'I can remember very clearly. And yet it's as though I've forgotten as well. As though it were the memory of someone else.'

'We must begin.'

'Hearing myself say that makes no sense. And yet it's all perfectly clear.'

'Focus on me and listen.'

'You?'

'Focus.'

'I know you.'

'Yes… you know me. Or you've known me before. In a different… environment.'

'We were close. I can sense that. A strong connection between us. Are we friends?'

'Let's go with that. Now – '

'What did we use to do?'

'Do?'

'Together.'

'All manner of things. Now listen, Max – '

'What?'

'I said, "Max". Does that mean anything to you?'

'I can see a woman crying. She's upset because I'm not… there. She's my wife, I think. Am I married?'

'To all intents and purposes.'

'Is she here?'

'No. Yes. Not in a way you would understand. At least not yet.'

'Are you…? No, no you're not. But you're connected to her in some way.'

'Yes.'

'I miss her.'

'That's… understandable. But not necessarily helpful. At the moment.'

'You.'

'Yes?'

'There's something different about you.'

'You're using senses that have been dormant for a while. That can cause a change in your perceptions.'

'You didn't use to talk like this.'

'Like what?'

'There's something… gentle about you now. Although, perhaps there always was. I just wasn't aware of it.'

'In one sense, you're waking up. There's a lot going on within you right now and this is something of a delicate stage. Some things may appear clearer than before, others less so or different – even radically different to what you knew. Or know.'

'I feel lighter.'

'That's good, that's quite normal.'

'But… I don't know. I feel I've been wasting time. Or not quite doing what I was supposed to. Concentrating too much on things that are less important than I thought. Not paying attention to… The answers were around me all the time, but I didn't take any notice. Or not enough notice. I was registering them and ignoring them at the same time.'

'Part of this process – an important part – is letting go of things, ideas you may have built up during this interim period of who you are. They can hold you back, hinder the process. Even reverse it, in some cases.'

'There's something unfinished.'

'There is always something unfinished.'

'Something I still have to do. A lot I still have to do.'

'Focus on me, on my voice, on this moment, here and now. I want you to think of nothing else. Just be with me, and listen to what I have to say.'

'There's something wrong.'

'What do you mean?'

'There's a fault – in the design.'

'There are no faults in the design.'

'Yes, I think I understand that. But I also know that you know what I'm talking about.'

'The choice I want you to make right now is to listen and focus on me. It's very important. Things will become even clearer as you do. Then you will understand fully. Right now there is still a powerful element of confusion in you, a deep wound pulling you away. Which is why you have to stay with me. Or the wound may consume you.'

'The wound.'

'I shouldn't have mentioned it. Forget it; it's past.'

'It's the reason I'm here.'

'And it no longer exists. It has served its function.'

'But others exist. Other people. Their wounds are real, happening right now.'

'You're becoming distracted. This oscillation is not sustainable. Which is why it is so important that you stay with me. Now, I need to run through some questions. Try to answer them as clearly as you can.'

'Questions? Are you a journalist?'

'Not exactly.'

'She's a journalist.'

'Who?'

'My wife. How can I know that? Is that a memory? I feel like I know so much and yet hardly anything at all. And there's so much more for me to understand.'

'You *will* understand.'

'And there it is again, that sense of not having used my time well. Like water slipping through my fingers, when I should be cupping it in my hands to drink.'

'More opportunities will come.'

'What, here?'

'Not here exactly.'

'I don't even know where I am. You haven't told me.'

'You're at the *Centro Paraíso*.'

'Sounds like a holiday resort. A tacky holiday resort.'

'It's a specialist centre for cases like yours.'

'I'm a 'case', am I?'

'Right now you're slipping away. We're in danger of losing this opportunity.'

'What if I want to go back? To where I was. You said this process could reverse.'

'I do not recommend that.'

'Why not?'

'In the vast majority of cases it leads to great instability, almost always irreparable. The risks are huge.'

'So it has happened.'

'Yes… But almost always ends badly. I've seen it myself.'

'But some have made it.'

'Some?'

'You said, "almost always". So there have been times when it's worked.'

'It's so rare as to be almost irrelevant. I have no reason to suspect that you would be one of those cases.'

'You don't believe that.'

'Sorry?'

'I know you don't believe what you just said. You're saying it because you feel you have to. You actually do think I could make it.'

'We have to start the interview. First question – '

'And do you know how I know that?'

'Go on.'

'Because it's what *you* always taught me to do. Don't give in, always keep going. Don't accept what they tell you lying down. Question everything. Find your own way forward. And above all, don't let anyone hold you back. It was a sort of family tradition.'

'So you did listen.'

'I know who you are now.'

'Good. It's a step, Max. Maybe not the right one, but an important one.'

'I'm not sure if I preferred you as you were before.'

'I'm still the same.'

'Yes… yes, I think you are. Inside. The outside is just… part of what gets left behind. I see that now. It's something else that moves on, something that was there all the time but hidden, like the sun behind a cloud.'

'Think you're a poet, now, do you?'

'Ha! There it is.'

'It never really goes away. I can call it up, if I want to.'

'Like putting on a fancy-dress costume.'

'You're being simplistic. It's more complicated.'

'I thought you were going to say that. See? I can read your mind.'

'Big deal. I've been reading yours since before you were born. Just like opening a book.'

'And you know what's going to happen next?'

'Yes, it's here on the page. That stubbornness runs deep. *Villano, terco y cazurro, nunca cae del burro* – You never see a villain, an idiot or a stubborn man fall off their donkey.'

'Well, you should know… So, what's it like here?'

'What's it *like*? It's not *like* anything. It just is. And you get on with it.'

'That's it. Fully back as you were. Crabby, sarcastic, bundle of laughs. Bet they loved it when you showed up.'

'Hey, you should see some of the others. I'm a fucking angel compared to them.'

'Angel, eh? And I never thought swearing would be allowed, either.'

'It's not a church, you know.'

'Thank fuck for that.'

'In fact, if there's one thing that dominates round here, it's laughter.'

'Laughter?'

'Not the nervous kind. Real laughter.'

'OK… I can't hear it.'

'That's because you're not fully here, you idiot. I'm trying to pull you through this but you keep slipping back.'

'Right. Yes, must concentrate. You keep telling me. It's not easy though, what with so much to take on. I mean, who'd have thought I'd bump into *you* here.'

'Well, it's not that unreasonable.'

'Don't get me wrong. I'm delighted, of course. I mean, I've missed you. Although in some ways it was as though you never really left. But I never knew you, you know, *believed* in this place.'

'Belief is overrated. It's only ever a stepping-stone.'

'You sound like a philosopher.'

'Because I fucking *am* a philosopher!'

'Right, yes, I suppose you are. All that stuff you used to spout about individual autonomy. There was a word we used to use to describe it. But I can't remember…'

'They're just words. They don't have much meaning now.'

'So these questions you keep mentioning. When are you going to start?'

'Oh, nice one. *You're* the one who's been holding us back... I don't think they're relevant any more.'

'No interview?'

'It's taking care of itself.'

'I've made my choice.'

'That's right.'

'And you know'.

'Why do you think I'm back to being like this?'

'Because it's coming from me?'

'Kind of. But don't get big ideas about yourself. Next thing you'll think the sun shines out of your arse. And that's how all the problems start.'

'Problems?'

'With the ones who don't stay. Get funny ideas about themselves, then they spiral out of control. Lost cases.'

'But not all of them. You said some manage to pull through.'

'Barely any at all, Max. You could practically count them on the fingers of one hand.'

'What do I have to do? To stay sane.'

'You've got to work that out for yourself.'

'Oh, thanks!'

'Look, you said before about ignoring the answers that were lying around you all the time. Well, stop ignoring them. Use them, work with them. Make them your own. You're meant to be a detective, aren't you? Well stop trampling over all the clues and start paying them the attention they deserve. Just because something doesn't have "CLUE" written all over it doesn't mean it's not important.'

'OK, I'll try.'

'Don't try. Do. Or you'll end up on the heap like so many others.'

'What happens to them?'

'You don't want to know. And I never want to see you there with them, understand?'

'What about the ones who do pull through. What do they do?'

'If you're worthy of it, you'll find out.'

'You know, it suits you, this place.'

'What do you mean?'

'You said it's filled with laughter.'

'It is.'

'Although I still can't hear any.'

'Trust me.'

'So, what better than to have a name like Hilario?'

'Go on, fuck off.'
'I will.'
'And don't expect me to be so friendly next time.'
'*Abuelo*?'
'What?'
'I love you.'
'So do I. Just don't fuck it up. Oh, and by the way, Max…'
'What?'
'This is going to hurt.'

ACKNOWLEDGMENTS

This book would never have got off the ground without the incredibly generous support of the following people, to whom I am extremely grateful: Peter Davies, Paul Berglund, Karole Webster, Mark Blandford, Lesley Coothoopermal, John Webster, Felicity Laughton, Patrick Dawson, Spike Golding, Tahir Shah, Agustín González, Holly Warton and Antonia Squire. Many thanks to all of you.

Salud, Arturo and Gabi have been the rock, as always, for the entire endeavour, and no words can do justice to the debt I owe them.

ABOUT THE AUTHOR

JASON WEBSTER was born in California to British parents in 1970 and spent his childhood in the US, Britain and Germany. He first moved to Spain in the early 1990s having graduated in Arabic and Islamic History from St John's College, Oxford. His many books on Spanish themes include *Duende: A Journey in Search of Flamenco; Guerra: Living in the Shadows of the Spanish Civil War*; a biography of the Spanish WWII double agent Garbo (*The Spy with 29 Names*); and the Max Cámara series of crime novels. The fifth of these, *A Body in Barcelona* (2015), predicted the Catalan independence crisis.

In 2011, Webster's short story, 'Rafaelillo' was included in *OxTravels*, a collection of pieces by twenty-five leading travel writers published in aid of Oxfam with an introduction by Michael Palin. In 2013 he presented 'Flashmob Flamenco', a documentary on BBC Radio 4 on the response within the Flamenco community to the economic crisis in Spain. He has appeared in TV documentaries for the BBC, Channel 5 and the Discovery Channel as an expert on Moorish Spain.

Webster is an award-winning photographer, co-founder of the Bridport School of Writing, and from 2014 to 2017 was the Flamenco correspondent for *Classical Guitar* magazine. From 2014 to 2017 he also created and led a series of cultural tours around Spain for the company Historical Trips, examining the history of the Pilgrimage to Santiago, relations between Moors and Christians in the Middle Ages, and the Spanish Civil War. The last of these was the first comprehensive tour of the conflict to exist and attracted considerable attention from the Spanish press; it was named as one of the best tours of Spain by the *Sunday Times*. In addition, Webster has written extensively for British and Spanish newspapers, including *The Financial Times, The Telegraph, The Guardian, The Observer, The Independent* and *El Asombrario*. He is married to the Flamenco dancer Salud and has two children.

www.jasonwebster.net

twitter.com/JWebsterwriter
facebook.com/jasonwebsterauthor

REQUEST

Good reviews are a great help

If you enjoyed this book, please review it on **Amazon**, **Goodreads**, or anywhere else you prefer.

If you'd like to know more about the author, please take a look at his website, www.jasonwebster.net

For Jason's popular blog 'Wit & Wisdom of Spain', please visit www.jasonwebster.net/wit-and-wisdom-of-spain

You can also subscribe to his Newsletter, including the free weekly *Pearls of Spanish Genius*